MW01031541

The Art of Forming
Young Disciples

EVERETT FRITZ

THE
ART OF
FORMING
YOUNG
DISCIPLES

Why Youth Ministries Aren't Working and What to Do about It

SOPHIA INSTITUTE PRESS
Manchester, New Hampshire

Copyright © 2018 by Everett Fritz

Printed in the United States of America

All rights reserved

Cover design by LUCAS Art & Design, Jenison, MI

No part of this book may be reproduced, stored in a retrieval system, or transmitted in any form, or by any means, electronic, mechanical, photocopying, or otherwise, without the prior written permission of the publisher, except by a reviewer, who may quote brief passages in a review.

Sophia Institute Press
Box 5284, Manchester, NH 03108
1-800-888-9344

www.SophiaInstitute.com

Sophia Institute Press® is a registered trademark of Sophia Institute.

Library of Congress Cataloging-in-Publication Data

Names: Fritz, Everett, author.
Title: The art of forming young disciples : why youth ministries aren't
    working and what to do about it / by Everett Fritz.
Description: Manchester, New Hampshire : Sophia Institute Press, 2018. |
    Includes bibliographical references.
Identifiers: LCCN 2017061604 | ISBN 9781622824823 (pbk. : alk. paper)
Subjects: LCSH: Discipling (Christianity) | Church work with youth—Catholic
    Church.
Classification: LCC BV4520 .F75 2018 | DDC 259/.23—dc23 LC record available at https://lccn.loc.gov/2017061604

First printing

*To my wife, Katrina: thank you
for all your love and support*

Contents

PART 3

The Twofold Solution

The Art of Forming
Young Disciples

Introduction

One afternoon, I was sitting at my desk, planning and preparing for an upcoming series of Sunday-night youth-group meetings. I had been working in parish youth ministry for nearly six years. I had a good number of teens participating in my group; I was doing consulting for several national youth-ministry organizations; and I was working at a large parish with a lot of resources at my disposal. I had everything that I believed I needed for a large, successful youth ministry.

Great worship band? Check.

Dynamic young adults trained as a core team? Check.

Dedicated youth space in the parish? Check.

Best youth-ministry resources and parish strategy that money can buy? Check.

Multiple full-time youth ministers on staff? Check.

Large budget? Check.

The youth ministry had grown exponentially since I had taken over as the director of the program. I was proud of what I had been blessed to accomplish in the Church. From the outside, youth ministry at the parish looked very successful.

That afternoon, however, my ideas about youth ministry began to change. I looked at a picture on my desk of a group of seventy-five teens I had taken to a big Catholic youth conference three years earlier. The conference had been a powerful experience for all the teens: they had had an encounter with Jesus Christ. I had stayed in contact with most of them because most of them had remained involved in my parish's youth group.

As I looked at that picture, it occurred to me that, out of the seventy-five teens, only ten were still practicing their Faith in college.

There was a story to go along with each fallen-away teen. Several of them had left the Faith due to their beliefs in liberal agendas (beliefs that their parents had raised them with); a few others had fallen victim to drugs and alcohol; others fell away due to promiscuity and bad relationships in which they had gotten into a habit of sin; and a few teens had never seemed to stand on a solid ground in their understanding of their Faith, making them easy prey for the secular agendas prevalent on college campuses.

I was deeply bothered by what I saw in that picture—so much so that I stopped planning my youth-group series and went to the chapel and prayed. That night, I couldn't sleep. There were too many questions running through my head.

What happened to all the teens who were in my youth ministry?

What am I doing wrong?

How can so many teens encounter Christ yet fail to become His followers?

What factors make the difference between a teen who becomes a lifelong disciple and a teen who falls away from the Church?

The Measure of Success

Two days later, I had lunch with a colleague in youth ministry. I told him how much our youth-group participation had grown in the last year and described the events that I had planned for the upcoming year. He asked me a question that caught me off guard because it echoed the questions I had been asking myself for a couple of days: "How many teens do you think will become lifelong disciples coming out of your youth ministry?"

I wasn't ready to admit that I had been wrestling with that question, so I started making excuses.

It's not about the numbers.

The parents are the real problem.

All teens are at different levels of development. Some are rich soil, while others are rocky or full of weeds.

In some cases, we're planting seeds that will take root later in a teen's life.

I was trying to provide context for my failure, because I knew the reality. After all, I had a lot of teens participating in my youth group. Most people in the Church would have said that my youth ministry was extremely successful.

But the teens were not becoming lifelong disciples—and that should be the *only* measure of success.

My friend pushed me harder: "Come on, quit making excuses. You know the teens in your program. How many do you think will be lifelong disciples?"

I swallowed hard and replied, "I know only about ten who I'm sure will become lifelong disciples. Please don't tell my pastor."

As if this embarrassment weren't enough, my friend pushed me harder: "What did you do differently with those ten that you didn't do with the other teens in your youth ministry?"

When I thought about it, those ten teens were the ones I had spent the most time with.

I did Bible study with them.

I mentored them in their prayer life.

I had a type of relationship with them in which I could challenge them to live virtuously.

I answered the difficult questions these teens had about the Faith.

I knew and mentored their parents.

I spent most of my relational ministry time with these teens.

When I described these criteria to my friend, he said, "*That's it!* That's the difference between success and failure with a teen. What you're describing to me is called *discipleship*—the process of mentoring someone through relationship and living example."

Then he asked me, "If that is the recipe for success, why don't you do that with every teen in your parish?"

And that's when it occurred to me what the problem in my ministry was. Why didn't I take the time to disciple every teen in the parish?

Because it would be impossible.

There is no way I could mentor every teen in the parish the way that I mentored those ten. It would take too much of my time, and I would be stretched too thin.

This is why youth ministry was failing in my parish: I had to think about the teens in my parish as one big group. In an effort to form all the teens in the Faith, I put on formation nights and activities for *all* the teens.

But teens need more than that.

In parishes, we try to *program* our teens instead of *mentoring* them. Teens need adult guidance and deep, meaningful relationships with other teens. And there is no possible way for one youth minister to meet the pastoral needs of every teen in the parish. Instead of thinking about the youth in the parish as one large group, I needed to think smaller. I needed to find a way to get on a mentoring level with every teen in the parish.

The 10,000-Hour Rule

I attended Catholic schools and Catholic youth groups, but I wouldn't credit either of those things with making me a disciple of Jesus Christ today.

When I had my first experience of Christ's love in my life (after having attended a retreat), I was ready to learn more about my Faith. The Faith and teachings of the Church were becoming real to me for the first time. I had a lot of questions and needed a lot of guidance—particularly in my prayer life.

Enter Fr. Brian Brownsey.

Fr. Brownsey noticed that Jesus had sparked a fire in my life. He took an interest in me as a person and offered me and several of my friends regular opportunities to grow closer to Christ and to get our questions answered. He made himself available for the sacrament of Reconciliation at all hours of the day and night. He took my friends and me to Eucharistic Adoration and then for ice cream after prayer. He offered to take me to lunch anytime to answer questions I had about the Faith—an opportunity I regularly took him up on. He always paid for meals, and he was always available. His invitation to grow closer to Christ was different from any invitation I had previously received. He didn't offer it as a general invitation from the pulpit. Rather, he pursued me personally and took an interest in understanding my life and my struggles. His attitude was: "I will do whatever it takes to help you grow into a lifelong disciple of Jesus Christ." His personal attention at that time made the difference between my thriving in my Faith and my leaving my Faith.

In *Outliers: The Story of Success*, author Malcolm Gladwell enunciates the "10,000-hour rule," which he discovered in studying people who have achieved world-class success and expertise in their fields. He found that the key to becoming a world-class expert is to practice the correct way of doing something for more than 10,000 hours.

Gladwell's theory has been called into question by some, but there is no doubt that the more time you spend at something, the better you become at it. In thinking about the premise of this book, and the problems facing young people in our Church today, I have considered Gladwell's "10,000-hour rule." Look at the way Jesus did ministry. He reached a lot of people with His ministry, but the people who went beyond Palestine to change the larger world were the apostles who lived with Him for three years. They spent more than 10,000 hours being personally mentored by God.

In the time I've spent in ministry, I've found that the young people to whom I've given the most attention are the ones who became lifelong disciples. It makes sense: imagine what the Church would look like if every person had 10,000 hours of mentoring.

But this seems impossible. After all, how do you spend that much individual time with each person in the Church? And how do you identify and empower enough mentors to give that much time to individuals?

The solution is easier than you think, but first we must have a good understanding of the different layers of the problems facing our young people today and why the Church has failed to address these problems.

PART 1

Understanding Youth Ministry

CHAPTER 1

We Are Losing Our Youth

Several years ago, I was sitting in a diocesan youth-ministry meeting. These monthly meetings were supposed to be for professional development. I can't say I got a whole lot out of them, but the free lunch was always delicious, so I would usually go if I didn't have anything more important to do.

At this meeting, the diocesan director told all the youth-ministry professionals that there would be an anniversary celebration for the diocese in the next year and that, as part of the celebration, we would have an event for the youth. I was excited about the prospect until I heard what we were doing: "We're going to have a walk-a-thon, with all of the teens walking down the main avenue of our city and raising money for a Catholic Charities after-school program."

This didn't sound like a good idea to me. Not only would the teens have to raise money for the diocese, but it was for a cause to which they had no strong commitment. I wondered how I was going to get teens excited to participate in this event.

A year later, when the event took place, I found the answer to my question. How did the diocese get the youth to attend? They mandated that every Catholic-school student participate — ensuring that well over a thousand students were there. Parish youth ministries enticed teenagers to attend by promising them service hours as part of their preparation for Confirmation. There were thousands of young people at the event, and they raised more than ten thousand dollars for Catholic Charities.

But it wasn't an event for youth. It was a public-relations stunt. The diocese got great publicity because of the event, and one of their ministries received much-needed funding from it.

There were thousands of Catholic teens in one place, celebrating being Catholic — except that they had no choice but to show up. They were at the event not because they were disciples of Jesus Christ who wanted to share their Faith with others but because they were required to be there. They were warm bodies — and nothing else. It didn't matter if they were disciples; in fact, one might wonder whether these young people had any interest in Catholicism at all.

This event typifies Catholic youth ministry in America: we are good at getting young people to participate. Our programs, events, and ministries do a good job — perhaps better than any other denomination in the world — at getting teens in the door.

Thousands of young Catholics attend World Youth Day every three years. Hundreds of thousands of teenagers in the United States attend Catholic youth conferences, mission trips, work camps, and Catholic camps. Hundreds of thousands are enrolled in Catholic youth programs in parishes every year (mostly for sacramental preparation).

To be fair, many of these events are excellent, with much better intentions than the diocesan walk-a-thon that I mentioned. But is participation alone a good indicator of success? Do we really have many, many young people who are being formed in Catholicism, ensuring the passing on of our Faith for generations to come?

Unfortunately, if we look just a little past the surface, the news is not good. In fact, Catholic youth ministry is a catastrophe.

Catholic Youth Ministry Is Not Working

In the United States alone, thirty million people identify themselves as "formerly Catholic," making up 10.1 percent of the national population.[1] The fastest-growing religious affiliation in the United States is "none." In a 2014 Pew Research Study, 36 percent of Americans in the eighteen-to-twenty-nine age range identified themselves as having "no religious affiliation." In fact, among the eighteen-to-twenty-nine age demographic in the United States, the "nones" now outnumber the Catholics. Nearly half of the "cradle Catholics" who become unaffiliated are gone by age eighteen. Seventy-nine percent are gone by age twenty-three.[2] When a soul walks away from the Church, that soul usually leaves when it is young.

Dynamic Catholic states that 85 percent of Catholic young adults stop practicing their Faith in college (most of them within their first year of leaving home).[3] Curtis Martin, the founder of the Fellowship of Catholic University Students (FOCUS) thinks that 85 percent is conservative, and that the Catholic Church

---

[1] Sherry A. Weddell, *Forming Intentional Disciples: The Path to Knowing and Following Jesus* (Huntington, IN: Our Sunday Visitor, 2012), 25.

[2] Ibid., 33.

[3] "Each year one million young Catholics are confirmed in the United States and 85% of them will stop practicing the faith within seven years of being confirmed." "Catholic Moments Confirmation Project," Who Is Matthew Kelly?, https://sites.google.com/site/whoismatthewkelly/.

is losing more than 90 percent of Catholic young people by the end of their college years.

This data isn't new. One can look at Dr. Christian Smith's *Soul Searching*[4] study from 2005 and see the same negative trends. In the 1990s, Mark DeVries of Ministry Architects tried to sound the alarm in evangelical churches that Christian youth were leaving those churches, too. The data has demonstrated the hemorrhaging for quite some time.

Recently I attended the expo of a large youth-ministry training conference. There were booths selling all kinds of resources and services for youth ministry: video resources, textbooks, parish programs, and youth-ministry books. There were recruiters for certification programs for youth ministry and for undergraduate and graduate degrees from major universities. There were booths with information about youth camps, conferences, mission trips, work camps, retreat centers, and events of every kind offered all over the country. There were speakers, musicians, and entertainers. There was Catholic music played everywhere, T-shirts for sale, and apps for iPhones. If you could think of it, it was there.

As I walked around the expo, one thought occurred to me: *if we are losing our young people in the Church today, it isn't due to lack of effort.* Nor is it due to a lack of good resources and programs. In fact, I really liked a lot of the products and services I saw offered at the expo. Lack of effort is not the problem.

Between the millions of dollars that the Church has invested in Catholic secondary education, and the time, talent, and treasure invested in youth ministry, young people get more attention

---

[4] Christian Smith and Melinda Lundquist Denton, *Soul Searching: The Religious and Spiritual Lives of American Teenagers* (Oxford: Oxford University Press, 2005).

from the Catholic Church than does any other ministry or demographic. Why is there so little return on that investment? More importantly, why is the Church failing to make young disciples?

Understanding Discipleship

One year, while I was a youth minister working in a parish, the parish hosted a mission intended to help Catholics dive deeper into Scripture. At the Sunday Masses, the speaker encouraged all the parishioners to come to his presentation on Monday night and to bring their Bibles. I took a handful of the teens in my youth ministry to the presentation. They all brought their Bibles, and we sat in the front row.

The speaker started the presentation by asking everyone to open their Bibles to a certain verse in the book of Leviticus. Virtually every adult sitting around us struggled simply to find the book in his Bible. I looked at my row of teens. Not only did they all have their Bibles open to the correct verse, but I noticed that every single one of the teens' Bibles was littered with handwritten notes, highlights, underlined verses, and sticky notes. All of their Bibles were worn and weathered because the teens had been reading and studying their Bibles.

In fact, their Bibles looked a lot like mine.

This is a simple example that demonstrates discipleship: the disciple imitates the rabbi.

I believe discipleship is marked by three characteristics: it is a process, it is an apprenticeship, and it involves practicing discipline.

Discipleship is a process

Much within our faith life operates as a process. We don't receive all the sacraments at once: they are conferred on us over the course of our lives. In the Rite of Christian Initiation of Adults (RCIA), a person goes through the stages of pre-evangelization, evangelization, conversion, catechesis, initiation, and mystagogia as he is initiated into the Catholic Faith.

In her book *Forming Intentional Disciples*, Sherry Weddell says that we need to return to our understanding of disciple making. She speaks of the five thresholds a person passes as he grows into intentional discipleship of Jesus Christ. The five thresholds are:

- *Initial trust*: A person is not practicing Catholicism, but has a positive association with Jesus Christ, His Church, the Blessed Virgin Mary, a person in the Church, or something else related to the Catholic Faith.
- *Spiritual curiosity*: A person is intrigued by Jesus Christ and desires to know more about Him and His Church but is not yet at a level of openness to life change.
- *Spiritual openness*: A person acknowledges to himself and to God that he is open to the possibility of personal and spiritual change (also known as conversion), but there is no commitment yet.
- *Spiritual seeking*: A person actively seeks to know the God who is calling him. He seeks to know and understand Christ and His Church.
- *Intentional disciple*: A person makes the decision to drop everything and follow Jesus.

Discipleship doesn't happen in an instant: it's an ongoing process in life.

Discipleship is an apprenticeship
In the days of Jesus, the word *discipleship* was used to describe the relationship between a student and a rabbi. As a young Jew grew up, he graduated from school to school. At the end of his

classroom education, he moved into the household of a rabbi, to live with him and learn from his way of life. When the student was old enough, the rabbi would either extend an invitation to him to "come after me" or tell him to "go and learn the trade of your father."

This is why Jesus extends the invitation to Peter, James, Andrew, and John to come and follow Him. They were plying the trade of their father; their opportunity to become disciples of another rabbi had come and gone, and they hadn't been chosen. Jesus, the greatest rabbi ever, gave each of these apostles a second chance.

As a disciple lived with a rabbi to learn from his daily example, so the apostles learned from the words of Jesus—from His words, yes, but even more from His manner of praying, the way He handled difficult situations, His daily routines, and His example. They knew Him intimately, and after He ascended into Heaven, they imitated His practices as the Church was born.

Discipleship is not discipleship without mentoring. A disciple must first be inspired to follow the rabbi and then be impacted by his living example. In discipleship, the Faith is not taught; it is caught. It is experiential in nature: the disciple learns by following the example of the rabbi.

Disciples practice disciplines

The words *disciple* and *discipline* come from the Latin word *discere*, "to learn." A disciple learns to be a disciplined person in everyday life. This means that disciples practice habits, and those habits lead to deeper conversion.

Most importantly, these practiced disciplines lead to a personal relationship with Christ—a relationship in which the disciple makes Jesus Christ the Lord and Savior of his life.

If a young person becomes a lifelong follower of Christ, the following habits will likely be visible in his life: regular visits to the Blessed Sacrament; weekly or even daily Mass attendance; daily prayer, including the Rosary; reading and studying Scripture; intentional growth in virtue and service; and tithing. This is what we want — to form our young people into lifelong followers of Jesus Christ and His Church through the process of discipleship.

Sounds simple, right?

The Crux of the Problem

Most people agree that there's a problem with youth ministry in the Church today, but there's very little consensus about what that problem is. Ask a person associated with the Church why youth ministry is struggling, and you will likely hear responses I have heard many times:

- A pastor will say that he lacks the funds necessary to hire a capable youth minister.
- A pastor will say that he can't find or keep a qualified youth minister.
- A youth minister will say that her pastor is not supportive.
- A parent will say that her teen doesn't like the youth group and doesn't connect with the youth minister.
- A youth minister will complain that parents are disengaged and aren't supportive of their teenagers' faith.
- A parent will complain that the Catholic school isn't doing a good job teaching the core doctrines of the Faith.
- A Catholic-school teacher will complain that parents are not modeling the Faith for their children at home.

- A parent will complain that the church youth group or religious-education program is little more than stale pizza, lame entertainment, and a boring curriculum.
- A parent will state that he is waiting for the pastor to fire the middle-aged DRE who is underqualified for working with young people and out-of-touch with modern methods of ministry.
- A diocesan director will observe that parish leadership lacks vision, so that teens end up planning their own ministry, or pastors and youth leaders end up pinning their hope of success on the latest program and resources.
- A bishop will observe that youth-ministry events in his diocese are all hype, flash, and entertainment, and no substance.
- A teenager will complain that the Church doesn't understand teens and that their questions about God and faith aren't being answered.

Any one of these statements may be true, but not a single one of them correctly identifies the problem in the Church today. These are symptoms of a greater problem: we don't understand young people and how to meet their most basic needs. If we don't understand the problem, we can never hope to solve it.

The best summary of youth ministry in our Church today comes from Pope Francis in his first apostolic exhortation, *Evangelii Gaudium*. He says:

Youth ministry, as traditionally organized, has also suffered the impact of social changes. Young people often fail to find responses to their concerns, needs, problems, and hurts in the usual structures. As adults, we find it hard to listen patiently to them, to appreciate their concerns, demands, and to speak to them in a language they can understand. For the same reason, our efforts in the field of education do not produce the results expected.[5]

The structures our Church uses to minister to young people are not meeting their basic needs, and because of this, our young people are failing to become disciples. It's not enough to have the best resources money can buy—a youth minister, a Catholic school—or to be catechizing a large number of teens. The landscape of youth culture is changing, but the Church has not adapted to these changes. In fact, in some cases, parishes are implementing approaches to youth formation that haven't been updated in more than four hundred years.

Our Church is facing a crisis—we are hemorrhaging young people. For decades, the Church has been talking of a New Evangelization—a kind of new birth or revolution of the gospel in the Church. But no major revolution in the world has ever thrived without a youth movement. The Church cannot reinvigorate her members so long as her young people are uninspired.

[5] Pope Francis, apostolic exhortation *Evangelii Gaudium* (November 24, 2013), no. 105.

CHAPTER 2

The Nature of Youth Ministry

Imagine that an island — previously uncharted and unknown — is discovered off the coast of Africa. On this island is an ancient tribe of cannibals with its own customs, music, dance, food, dress, value system, and way of life.

Taking seriously the call to go and make disciples of all nations, the Catholic Church decides to send missionaries to this island to share the gospel of Jesus Christ and to provide catechesis for the members of this tribe. Four missionary priests fly to Africa and take a boat to the island. They are equipped with Bibles, a *Catechism of the Catholic Church*, everything they need to celebrate the liturgy, rosaries, and several prayers in Latin that they can distribute to teach the tribe members how to pray.

When they make contact with the tribe, the four missionary priests immediately identify the chief of the cannibal tribe and approach him. They briefly give the reason they are on the island and explain to the chief that cannibalism is wrong and that they are going to set up weekly classes to teach the members of the tribe about the Catholic Faith. They distribute the Latin prayers and invite the members of the tribe to join them for the celebration of the Holy Mass.

What's going to happen to those missionaries?

The cannibal tribe is going to eat them for dinner.

But why?

The missionaries don't know anything about the tribe. They don't know how to speak their language. The tribe has no reason to trust their message. The missionaries don't understand what the tribe values, and because of that, they can't communicate effectively. Without trust, a common language, and shared values, the only importance that the missionaries serve for the tribe is to provide them with their next meal.

The goal of any good missionary is not to become dinner. The goal of a good missionary is to *be invited* to dinner. In sharing a meal with the people they seek to serve, missionaries can learn from them and can gain the skills necessary to learn to communicate with them.

What Is Youth Culture?

Replace "cannibal tribe" with "American teenager," and you may begin to understand what youth ministry is supposed to be. A culture is the way of life of a people — what they value, how they communicate, how they dress, their music, dance, and customs. In recent years, there has been a lot of talk in the Church about the development of a "youth culture" in America. But, what is "youth culture"?

Prior to the industrial revolution, the world and professions were much less complicated. Children would typically go straight from childhood into the adult workforce — learning the trade of their parents. Higher education was not an option for most young people. As the workforce became more complex, more education became necessary in order for young persons to progress in the workforce. This meant that young people stayed in school longer, and a period of development known as adolescence became common. Teenagers in school were not yet adults but were also no longer children.

After World War II, for the first time in human history, a "culture" started to develop around teenagers. America had left behind the Great Depression and wartime economics, and the country was booming economically. The newest form of media—the television—became commonplace in every home. The G.I. Bill made it possible for more people than ever to attend college (again postponing young people's entry into the workforce and independence).

Around this time, companies discovered that American teenagers were a marketable demographic, and products began to be mass-produced and -marketed to teenagers instead of to their parents. As a result, teenagers began to have hairstyles, a way of speaking, clothes, music, values, and ideals that were different from those of their parents. A different culture developed around youth. That culture impacted the people they would become.

As youth culture—still in its early stages of development—grew into the 1960s, young people worldwide experienced several revolutions. The sexual revolution, the rock 'n' roll revolution, the drug revolution, and anti-authority movements were all born from youth movements. At around the same time, the Catholic Church was going through the confusing times of Vatican II. Young people became characterized by their music, their anti-authority rebellion, their rampant drug abuse and sexual promiscuity, the way they dressed, talked, and looked, and even their suspicion of religion. Since then, not much has changed. That's because the "culture" that developed out of this time has largely influenced the upbringing and development of young people over the past several decades.

We cannot look at teenagers in the world today and say, "They have always been rebellious, anti-religious, and lacking in virtue. That's just part of being a teenager." That isn't true — it hasn't always been the case. Teenagers today are different from teenagers of several hundred years ago. They are different even from teenagers of just a few decades ago.

An interesting fact about youth culture is that its ideals, styles, language, and trends are constantly changing. A generation of teenagers lasts only about seven years, and each new one seeks to differentiate itself from the previous generation. Things change rapidly in youth culture — and therefore efforts in evangelizing and discipling teens have to change as well in order to maintain effectiveness.

In our Church today, we cannot say, "Let's rely on methods the Church used several decades ago, when the seminaries were full and teens were more virtuous." These methods won't work with teenagers today. We're dealing with a different culture, which necessitates a constant missionary approach in order to be effective.

What Is a Missionary?

A missionary's job is to evangelize a *culture* with the gospel of Jesus Christ. But missionaries do not do this merely by setting up classes and communicating dogmas and traditional prayers. As we saw with the example of the cannibals, this is not typically an effective approach for evangelization.

A missionary spends time in a culture to gain that culture's trust. A missionary gains trust by building relationships. In building relationships, the missionary earns the right to be heard. Also, by building relationships with the people, the missionary learns the culture's language and values—which, in turn, helps the missionary to communicate the gospel.

Relational ministry is what Jesus did. He wanted to evangelize all of mankind, so He became one of us. God became man and used our language and our values to communicate with us. He lived among us and gained our trust. He taught using parables and examples that the people of His time would understand.

A missionary doesn't seek to create cookie-cutter Catholic cultures. Rather, he seeks to *baptize* particular cultures, identifying the good within them and using understood values to elevate them to an understanding and acceptance of the teachings of Catholicism. This is why the customs of Africa, Asia, Europe, and America are all incorporated into the life of the Church. If you go to any of these continents, the celebration of Catholicism might look different, yet it's all essentially the same. The Church is universal because she draws all of us into her way of life.

The same can be said for youth culture. In order for youth ministry to be successful, we must learn to listen to young people—to their values, worries, and way of life—and where possible, we must find ways to teach and baptize into Catholicism what they value. Merely setting up classes to teach traditional prayers will never be effective in evangelizing the modern-day teenager. Missionaries are necessary.

Catholic missionaries are successful when they have deeply rooted habits of prayer. Just as young people adopt the fashions and language of modern pop icons they admire, so will they eventually follow and emulate a saintly missionary. If a missionary has a strong prayer life, so will the person who seeks to emulate him.

Once a missionary achieves a relationship with another person, the relationship has become ministry.

What Is Ministry?

I was busy setting up a diocesan youth-ministry presentation when two young women arrived early. I introduced myself, and we got into a conversation.

One of the women was a youth-ministry intern at her parish. She had been part of her parish youth group and had stayed involved as a volunteer while working on her degree at a local community college.

I asked her, "How's the youth ministry going at your parish?"

She replied, "The ministry is going great. The youth group's involvement had dwindled over the past couple of years, but recently we've been working hard, and now our youth group has grown to over forty teens!"

"That's great. What are you doing in your parish to minister to the teens?"

"We've been inviting teens and working with some new programs and resources. It's been really great to see the teens coming each week and enjoying their Faith!"

"I see. So … what are you doing to *minister* to the teens?"

"Each week, we start with pizza and a game, and then we do some teaching and prayer with the teens."

"That sounds like a good structure. But what are you doing to *minister* to the teens?"

She looked confused. I wasn't getting through to her.

Ministry is the process of meeting a person's pastoral needs. This is an extremely important concept. It's not enough to have a curriculum, resources, structure, volunteers, participation, and events. If youth ministry at the parish doesn't meet a young person's primary pastoral needs, then youth ministry is not happening.

To make disciples, we must form people intellectually, spiritually, and as human persons. To minister to a person, we must identify his needs as they relate to each of those categories. This requires individualized attention. Every individual has pastoral needs, and when a person lacks relationships with mentors and like-minded peers in his church, he lacks the relationships that are necessary to meet his individualized needs.

If success is measured by making disciples, then our ministry has to start with a plan for meeting the individualized needs of each young person.

Unfortunately, youth ministry has become a series of programs and events intended to keep kids in the Church in hopes that we won't lose them. If we have any hope of stopping the loss of our youth, we must start at the source of the problem and meet the basic pastoral needs of each person.

CHAPTER 3

Understanding the Needs of Every Teen

It was nearly 1:00 a.m., and I was sitting in an empty restaurant just off the hotel lobby across from a broken, hurting seventeen-year-old girl.

I was at a youth conference in Florida, and members of my youth group were in their hotel rooms for the night. We had just had a powerful evening of prayer, Eucharistic Adoration, and empowerment, and the teens in my group were buzzing. We had had our standard small-group discussions after the experience, and I said, "If any of you still has something that God did in your heart tonight—something you need to talk about—I'll sit here in the hotel lobby for a while, and we can talk it out." Sure enough, I had several teens take me up on the offer. Around 1:00 a.m., I thought I was done talking and could finally go to bed, when Julia came around the corner and approached me.

"I need to talk," she said. I could tell it was important.

"Okay. Let's grab a seat in this empty restaurant," I responded.

As soon as we sat down, Julia blurted out, "I can't stop drinking."

I knew a little about Julia's background before I took her to the youth conference. She was a high school senior who got drunk at parties nearly every weekend, had experimented with drugs, and had a reputation for being promiscuous. I think she even showed up for the youth conference hung over.

On the other hand, Julia was a sweet, wonderful girl, very beautiful, artistic, and full of good intentions. It didn't take me long in our conversation to realize that she had encountered Jesus in a powerful way that evening and was wrestling with her sin and brokenness. However, the conversation went in a direction I wasn't expecting.

I said to her, "There are a lot of people who have wrestled with addiction. The first step is to admit the problem and to come closer to Jesus."

She interrupted me: "I'm not an addict. I would have no problem giving up drinking. I know that is what Jesus wants me to do, and I'm ready to do it. I don't even like getting drunk. The problem is, I can't leave my friends."

That caught me off guard. As we talked, I got more of Julia's background story. Her parents were divorced. Her father was absent but knew about her partying and promiscuity and didn't care, and her mother wasn't present emotionally. Her brother was in rehab. She said, "The only people in my life who love me are my friends, and they all party. If I stop, I'll lose them."

This is not the conversation I was expecting. I told her that anyone who was a real friend would love her, not for her sharing vices with them, but because of who she was. I prayed with her and told her that Jesus would help her find her way. I encouraged her to keep coming to youth group to grow in a community of friends who were virtuous. We ended in prayer, but I could tell that she didn't have total confidence that her needs would be met following the conference.

Unfortunately, the story doesn't end well.

I can't fault Julia: she gave it her best. She came to youth group every week and tried to participate. I saw her, by herself, at Mass every Sunday. I followed up with her regularly and tried to encourage her. It didn't matter—the youth group was not right for her. She never quite fit in, and the group wasn't help-ing her to feel confident that she ever would. With every game, skit, video clip, catechetical talk, and prayer exercise, she would try, but I saw her drifting further and further away. Eventually, she began coming only every other week, then occasionally, and finally not at all. I reconnected with her almost a year after her initial encounter with Christ at the conference. She had fallen back into the same sins and lifestyle that she had before the conference, and she was no longer interested in a relationship with Jesus Christ or His Church.

Julia had tried—and she had even articulated the problem. She had basic needs that had to be met for her to become a life-long disciple. Unfortunately, the structure of ministry I had put into place was not sufficient to meet her basic needs.

Meeting Teens' Basic Needs

If I had to answer in one sentence "Why are young people leav-ing the Catholic Church?," I would respond, "The Church is not meeting the basic needs of young people."

American psychologist Abraham Maslow is most famous for his theory of a "hierarchy of needs," which basically claims that unless a person's innate needs are met, he will never become psychologically and spiritually complete.

Think about this theory for a second.

If you were stranded on a desert island, your first thought would probably not be about getting off the island. Instead, you'd need to find food, water, shelter, and fire. Once those basic needs were met, you'd turn your attention to self-actualization—which, in this case, would be getting off the island.

We can say the same thing about teenagers in our Church. Why is it that so many are not becoming lifelong disciples of Jesus Christ? Because their basic needs are not being met by our Church structures.

This was my problem with Julia—she wanted to grow to the point of self-actualization (in her case, breaking free of sin and following Christ completely), but she couldn't, because our youth ministry was not meeting her basic needs.

So, what are the basic needs of a young person?

My colleague Sean Dalton at the Augustine Institute in Denver articulates better than anyone the five basic needs of teens: the need to be understood, the need to belong, the need to be transparent, the need for critical thinking about faith and life, and the need for guidance.[6] Let's look at each of those basic needs.

The need to be understood

In my first year as a youth minister, I struggled to connect with the teens I was serving. The program I had started in a parish was failing miserably. I visited family in Chicago for Christmas and spent that time away from the parish wrestling with what I was doing wrong in my ministry. My wife suggested that we visit a friend of ours who was serving as a missionary in Chicago with an organization called Emmaus Ministries.

Catholics in Emmaus Ministries work with male prostitutes on the streets of Chicago. They own a house close to the "gay

---

[6] Augustine Institute, "5 Fundamental Needs of Teenagers," in *YDisciple Handbook* (Denver: Augustine Institute, 2015), 5.

bar" district in Chicago (commonly known as Boystown), and they send missionaries into the streets late at night in order to build relationships with the male prostitutes. The missionaries invite the prostitutes to come to the house for a meal, a shower, or other basic needs. Once at the house, the missionaries work to build relationships with the men, to get them off the street, and to rehabilitate them through Bible study, counseling, drug rehabilitation, and job training.

While I was visiting my friend, he asked if I wanted to do an "immersion night," which was how visitors were introduced to the work of Emmaus Ministries. When I agreed, I thought I was just going to shadow the missionaries as they went out into the streets that evening. Little did I know what my friend had in mind: an immersion night consisted of going gay-bar hopping.

The rules were simple: my group was not allowed to talk about God or our Faith, and our goal was to learn from the people we met. At first, I wondered how I had gotten roped into this exercise, and I was extremely uncomfortable; but in one bar, I struck up a conversation with a construction worker from the suburbs. During the conversation, I realized what the evening was supposed to teach me: "If I don't first understand the people I am ministering to, I can never hope to reach them with the gospel. Every person has a cross in his life, and the first step in helping someone to accept Christ's love is to help him to carry his cross."

Emmaus Ministries was very wise in setting up these exercises for those interested in joining their ministry. They wanted all their missionaries to understand that Christ spent less time judging sinners and more time walking alongside them, loving them back to health. The purpose of this exercise was to teach missionaries to see each person for who he is—someone created in the image and likeness of God.

The same could be said of teenagers in our Church today. Too many ministries in parishes approach teens with the intention of teaching them about the Faith without first seeking to know them. When I grasped this principle—that the people we minister to must first be understood—my entire approach to youth ministry changed. Teenagers don't care how much you know until they know how much you care. Before you teach them about the Faith, you must earn the right to be heard.

The need to belong

Every person has a need to belong with other people. After all, we're made for love, and because of that, we seek out relationships. Teenagers, however, have such a strong need to belong that *they will sacrifice the moral values that they are raised with in order to belong.*

Think about it—why do teens get involved in gangs, drugs, drinking, sex, and other sinful activities? Because they find a sense of belonging with the people who do these activities.

Parents understand better than anyone their teens' need to belong. This is why so many parents are willing to overcommit their teenagers to so many activities—so their teenagers will find community and belonging. Parents know that if they don't get their teenagers' need to belong met, their teens may find a sense of belonging in a community that they don't want them to be a part of.

As a youth minister, I frequently had trouble with parents who prioritized their teens' extracurricular activities ahead of my youth-ministry program or the sacramental formation requirements of my parish. In my early years as a youth minister, I was frustrated by this constant battle with parents to prioritize the faith formation of their children. It wasn't until I had my own kids that I began to understand better how parishes put parents between a rock and a hard place.

When parents prioritize their kids' extracurricular activities ahead of faith formation, what they essentially are saying to the parish leadership is that *their children find a greater sense of belonging within their extracurricular activities than they do in the Church.* That means that the parish is at fault: the parish is failing to meet the children's basic needs. In these cases, when parish leadership insists that teens participate in the parish faith formation (or else, for example, they will be unable to receive a sacrament), the parish puts the parents in a difficult position. Do the parents put their children in the parish formation program, where their kids will not feel as if they belong? Or do they keep them on the soccer team with all their friends? More times than not, the Church loses that battle.

I spoke with a friend who had this exact problem. Her daughter was preparing for Confirmation. Her daughter was very well formed in her Faith and grew up in a family with strong, faithful parents. The parents had done an exceptional job raising and modeling the Faith to their children. But Confirmation classes in the parish conflicted with dance-team rehearsals, and the parish offered the classes only once per week. When the parent objected to the mandatory classes and the lack of flexibility, the parish leaders informed her that she simply wasn't putting the Faith first in her child's life.

When I spoke with this parent about her frustrations with this, I asked where her daughter found friendships and fellowship more easily—with her dance team or with the kids in the parish. The parent said, "With her dance team. My daughter doesn't like the parish youth group." We discussed the matter at length, and you can guess which activity the parent chose to prioritize—the dance team. The reason: her daughter had a basic need to belong, and that's where she found belonging. The parent found an alternative path to get her child the sacraments.

We cannot expect teens to become lifelong disciples unless we create an environment (or environments) in which teens can develop friendships with other teens and find a sense of belonging in our parishes.

The need to be transparent

One in six high school students has considered suicide. One in twelve has attempted suicide.[7] Every person carries a cross in his life. Some crosses are heavier than others. If you don't have a place you can go or a person you can talk to when you have trouble in your life, you internalize that problem.

One thing I have noticed in my ten years of working with teenagers is the superficiality of their relationships. Many teens do not have friends with whom they can be transparent. With boys, especially, most of their friendships revolve entirely around shared interests—such as sports or video games. Often, if a teenager is having difficulty with something in his life, he doesn't have anyone he feels he can approach about that problem—and about his subsequent emotions.

After my experience at Emmaus Ministries, I spent the better part of the remainder of my first year of youth ministry focusing on developing relationships with teens I met. Although the quality of my program still needed work, the quality of my relationships with teens gradually improved. Teens make you work for

---

[7] Meghan Neal, "1 in 12 Teens Have Attempted Suicide," *Daily News*, June 9, 2012, http://www.nydailynews.com/life-style/health/1-12-teens-attempted-suicide-report-article-1.1092622.

their affection, but once they find that you are willing to listen to their problems, to treat them with respect, and to offer them help, they become an open book.

About twelve months after I started focusing on growing relationships with teens in my parish, I could have opened a counseling practice. I had more teens sharing their struggles with me than I knew what to do with.

Every teen is a person, and every person carries a cross. All teens have a basic need to be transparent, because if they can't be transparent about their struggles, they'll never learn how to surrender their cross to Christ. I have learned that the Church has to provide the right context for teens to be transparent. Otherwise, teens don't grow into disciples.

The need for critical thinking about the Faith

Believe it or not, teenagers are fascinated by faith-related topics. Teens have a lot of questions about faith and religion, and they want answers to their questions. The Catholic Church does a fantastic job of answering questions that teens *do not have* but does not do a good job of answering the questions that teens *do have*.

On Sundays, most teenagers enter a church where the message communicated from the pulpit has little relation to their life (actually, that's the experience of most Catholics in general). In faith-formation classes, most teens endure a pre-determined curriculum that systematically walks them through the dogmas of the Creed and the *Catechism*. Sometimes, they experience a pre-determined curriculum that is disjointed, with no scope and sequence at all. Seldom does a teenager experience formation in his faith that grows organically out of the natural questions he has.

Children believe anything that a trusted adult tells them. This is why kids believe in Santa Claus—because they trust their parents, and they believe anything their parents tell them. The same is true of children and catechesis in the parish. When they're young, children accept basic instruction in Church teachings because their parents or catechists tell them that those teachings are true. You can tell a child that God and Heaven exist, and he believes it without question.

As children enter adolescence, their minds develop the capacity for critical thinking, and they begin to question whether what is being taught is true. They begin to separate their thinking from adults and to ask themselves, "Do I believe this to be true?" This is good. It's part of the process of becoming an adult. This is what causes a child eventually to start to question Santa Claus and to think rationally. At some point, a child begins to think, "It doesn't make sense that there is a man at the North Pole who lives on a diet of milk and cookies and travels in a flying sleigh with magical reindeer to every house in the world, delivering presents while going up and down chimneys. This doesn't seem rational."

Naturally, as children enter adolescence and their minds develop critical-thinking capabilities, they begin to ask, "Do I believe that God and Heaven exist? Do I believe what my family and teachers have taught me?" They develop questions about faith and even challenge some of the things they have been taught. This is good. They are engaging in critical thinking. It's the beginning of their taking ownership of their faith.

Unfortunately, too often the method of teaching and engaging teens in the parish does not change as children grow into adolescence. Too often, the Church expects teens simply to accept what is communicated to them. If they don't receive good answers to their questions, teens begin to believe that the Church *doesn't have* good answers because good answers *don't exist*. They become disengaged in church and begin to reject the dogmas of the Church in favor of the dogmas of their youth culture. Eventually, as these teens enter adulthood, they stop attending church altogether.

Teens need relationships, and, within those relationships, they have to be given the opportunity to engage in critical thinking and discussions about faith and life. If that basic need is not met, they will not become disciples.

The need for guidance

Adolescence is a difficult time for young people. Their minds and bodies are changing. They're becoming interested in, and many times pursuing, relationships with the opposite sex. They face decisions about vocation, education, and occupation—decisions that will affect the rest of their lives. They face peer pressure, pressure to abuse drugs and alcohol, identity questions, and pressure to excel in school. They are transitioning into adulthood. If there were ever a time when persons were in need of guidance, it's during adolescence.

Now, think about the schedule of American teenagers. They wake up early in the morning and rush out the door to school. They spend eight or nine hours a day in a classroom surrounded by peers, with a teacher who needs to communicate an enormous amount of content to them in a short time. After school, teenagers usually rush off to an extracurricular activity or an after-school job. When they come home, sometimes their parents are home, and sometimes they're not. Maybe they'll have dinner with the family, but many times they probably won't. Then they retire to their room, where they do two or three hours of homework and go to sleep.

Looking at the schedule of the average American teenager, consider this important question: *At what point during most teenagers' daily schedules do they have a meaningful conversation with an adult?*

Most teens don't have adults who provide guidance in their lives. In this period when teens are most in need of guidance, our culture has removed from their lives the very people who are responsible for providing guidance. The average schedule for an American teenager does not allow for mentoring relationships with adults. As a result, when teenagers need advice, they're more likely to turn to a peer than to an adult because they have relationships with their peers and no relationship with adults.

I believe that the need for guidance is the most important of these five needs. The Church cannot expect to form teens into disciples without meeting their basic need for guidance.

The Problem of Context

Pope Francis also believes that youth ministry in our Church is not meeting teens' basic needs. Without that, we can't expect them to grow into disciples — they'll never move to the point of self-actualization.

If we want our youth to stop leaving the Church, we need to change our approach. The next three chapters aim to identify how each of the most common formation practices in our culture and in our Church is failing to meet the most basic needs of teens.

Too often, the Church recognizes that teens cannot clearly articulate beliefs about faith and religion. The Church responds by trying to adjust and improve her delivery of *content* to teenagers. As a result, we see the influx of resources — social media resources, video-based resources, conferences, and rallies for teens — that are intended to communicate the Faith better on the level of a teenager. We now have tremendous content resources in our Church — better than we've had in a long time.

Unfortunately, the greatest problem in youth ministry in our Church today is not *content* but *context*. We're not creating an environment in which teens can have their basic needs met: the need to be understood, to belong, to be transparent, to engage in critical thinking, and to find guidance. As a result, they're not becoming lifelong disciples.

PART 2

The Catholic Youth-Ministry Problem

CHAPTER 4

The Cultural Problem: The Separation of Youth from Adults

In 2015, the highest-grossing summer blockbuster movie was *Jurassic World*—the fourth installment of the popular dinosaur-meets-man series. In this movie, Jurassic Park had become a great success, and people came from all over the world to see and participate in the dinosaur zoo experience. The problem was that the park struggled to come up with new attractions, and the costs of developing and maintaining dinosaur life was expensive.

As a solution, the dinosaur embryologists decided to cross-breed a Tyrannosaurus rex with a velociraptor to create a new dinosaur. Owen, the person in charge of caring for and training the velociraptors, was horrified to discover that this experiment had taken place, and he rebuked the scientists for their irresponsibility. Sure enough, the newly created Indominous rex escaped from its cage and went on a killing spree in the park—resulting in another dinosaur-versus-man drama.

One bit of dialogue in the movie stands out. Owen is angry when he discovers that Indominous rex is raised in isolation from other dinosaurs. He says, "You're raising this dinosaur in a world it doesn't belong in, and you're keeping it isolated from the world you expect it to participate in." When the dinosaur escapes, it turns violent because it doesn't know how to assimilate into a world that it doesn't understand.

This describes the cultural problem that teenagers face in the modern world. We expect them to learn to participate in the world of adults, but our culture has largely removed adults from mentoring roles with teenagers. As a result, teens are growing up in a peer-dominated culture. As they grow into adulthood, they have difficulty assimilating into the adult world and into the responsibilities and expectations that come with being an adult.

The results are not good. More and more millennials move back home after completing college, failing to find motivation to get a job and to begin to develop a career. Young adults are running from the lifelong commitment of marriage and family and are instead choosing the hookup culture—moving from one sexual relationship to the next, without any commitment to the person with whom they are intimate. Young adults even turn violent—toward others or even themselves. I often wonder how much violence in schools would be eliminated if teens had adult mentors in their lives.

"They Have No Clue"

In *Hurt 2.0: Inside the World of Today's Teenagers*, Dr. Chap Clark speaks to this problem, which he refers to as "systemic abandonment":

> In all societies since the beginning of time, adolescents have learned to become adults by observing, imitating, and interacting with grown-ups around them.... It is therefore startling how little time [modern] teenagers spend in the company of adults. One study found that

adolescents spent only 4.8% of their time with their parents and only 2% with adults who were not their parents.[8]

Dr. Clark goes on to explain that we absolutely cannot make the mistake of thinking that very little has changed in the world of teenagers over the last several decades. The world of teenagers has changed and continues to change—and not for the better. One need only walk through the hallways of a high school on any given day and overhear the conversations of students. The things discussed and the environment of the school are much more juvenile and dangerous than they were several decades ago.

Dr. Clark surveyed and studied teenagers for several years. He discovered an underworld within high school culture—devoid of adults and guidance. He observed a tribal survivalist mentality among cliques in the school. Teens spoke of their feeling of separation from their family and teachers. There is unhealthy pressure and competition to stand above their peers in sports and academics. Finally, he encountered an oversexualized subculture—one in which teens had their own language and communication about sex, and they were neither surprised nor morally opposed to any kind of sexual behavior (no matter how compulsive or deviant).

This is not the environment of previous generations. The peer-dominated world of today's youth struggles with suicide, self-worth and identity, dangerous sexual attitudes, unhealthy stress and expectations, and addictions to social media and gaming. What's more, Dr. Clark found that teens believe that their parents are unaware of the struggles in their life. One teenage girl said that her parents were oblivious to her depression and

---

[8] Chap Clark, *Hurt 2.0: Inside the World of Today's Teenagers* (Grand Rapids, MI: Baker Academic, 2011), 38.

self-hatred. She said, "They have no clue." She was an all-league volleyball player, maintained a 4.0 grade point average, and was well-liked at school. She was good at "playing the game"—looking as if she had it all together. Meanwhile, the tribal culture in her high school was destroying her life.

Lord of the Flies

Many of us read *Lord of the Flies* in high school. The book is similar to *Jurassic World*. Kids are stranded on a desert island after their plane crashes. All the adults have died in the crash. The kids setup a "tribal" culture in order to have hierarchy, authority, and structure on the island. Eventually, the tribe turns on its weaker members and resolves to kill one of them. At the end of the book, right before they are going to kill their peer, a military officer shows up. He had discovered the crash and is there to rescue the children. When the kids see the adult, they drop their weapons and break down crying. Proper order is restored—the children have an adult in their life whom they can look to for guidance.

We are led to believe that teenagers don't want adults in their lives. Movies and television that are marketed to teenagers rarely show parents in a positive light. Parents are either absent from the movies entirely or are portrayed as aloof and out of touch.

American culture has isolated young people from their parents and from adult guidance. From the time they begin kindergarten, children spend a large part of their day away from their parents. As they grow older, their education is devoted to teaching them specific information—advanced mathematics, computer science, and so forth. Athletics has become specialized as well, focusing on the science behind being a better athlete. It's rare to find adults who focus on mentoring as a primary part of their job as a teacher, coach, or employer. Teaching virtue to young people has become a lost priority.

Home is no better. A recent survey shows that the average American family spends less than eight hours together each week.[9]

So what happens when adults don't provide necessary guidance? Teens grow up in a peer-dominated culture. They spend the majority of their time in large-group environments with classmates, and they turn to their classmates for advice when they need it. This results in poor life decisions because the blind are leading the blind (see Matt. 15:14).

Children Yearn for Parental Involvement

The perception in our culture is that young people do not want relationships with adults or parents. Yet *USA Today* surveyed 1,200 teenagers, and 76 percent of them said that they *wanted* their parents to spend more time with them.[10] Young people are craving adult guidance; and like the kids on the island in *Lord of the Flies*, emotional walls and barriers come down when proper order is restored to a young person's life.

In ministry, I see this effect all the time. I joke that my left shoulder is always soggy from the number of tears that teens have cried there. Recently I was speaking with a friend who works in college ministry. She told me that on her first day back on campus for the spring semester, she would get hammered with

---

[9] SBrinkmann, "Survey: Families Spend Less Than 8 Hours Together Per Week," *Women of Grace* (blog), July 16, 2013, http://www.womenofgrace.com/blog/?p=22778.

[10] Mark DeVries, *Family-Based Youth Ministry*, 2nd ed. (Downers Grove, IL: InterVarsity Press, 2004), 41.

requests from students for "coffee dates." She said, "Last year I counted. From the time I left my office to the time I reached my car (a three-hundred-foot walk), I had *twelve* students approach me and ask to meet with me for private coffee dates."

I have another friend in college ministry who told me that she has students knocking on her door and sitting on her couch almost every night of the week. She jokes that she keeps buckets of cookie dough from Costco on hand because she knows there are going to be college students at her house every night. "I tell them to open their mouth, and I shovel in the cookie dough."

Teens need adult mentors in their lives.

So, how do we fix this problem? Is the crux of the problem the parents? Can we blame parents for not providing adult guidance in a young person's life? If so, how does this translate to ministry?

Parents Are the Primary Educators

The Catholic Church teaches that parents are the primary educators of their children. Yet, speaking with those who work in religious education, I find a universal frustration with parents. The consensus is that parents are not doing a good job fulfilling their role as the catechists of their children. There is plenty of merit to this frustration, but I don't entirely agree that parents are failing in their responsibility.

The word *primary* can be translated as "first." We could say that parents are the first educators of their children when it comes to the Faith. Speaking with a friend of mine who is a Catholic psychologist, I lamented that I didn't think I was doing a good job raising my three young children in the Faith. He told me something that changed my perspective on the meaning of *primary educators.*

My friend said, "My clients generally express some sort of dissatisfaction with their parents and their upbringing. Interestingly, their issue with their parents, particularly their father, usually parallels their perception of who God is. If their parents were strict disciplinarians, they tend to view God as someone who punishes you if you break the rules. If their parents were absent in their lives, they believe that God is absent, too. If their parents were timid or overbearing, again there is a parallel. But if their parents loved them unconditionally, they don't have a problem understanding that our God loves them unconditionally. The best thing you can do to raise your young children in the Faith is to love them the way that God loves us—unconditionally."

All of a sudden, the fact that my kids didn't have the right prayers memorized or hadn't mastered their catechism lessons didn't matter as much to me. I realized that my love for them as a father was going to witness God the Father to them. My example of love was the first lesson they would learn about God the Father. If I did not witness love to them, they would not grow up with faith.

I believe that parents don't fail as primary educators as much as we think. Most parents I know are not theologians, and all of them are sinners. But I know many parents who love their children. And if parents know how to love their children, then the Church can and should build off this example to teach a child the gospel.

I have found that parents who love their children are more motivated than anyone else to meet their children's pastoral needs. Yet parents of teenagers are often burned out and can be uncertain about what to do with their teenagers. Many parents who do not consistently attend Mass have been hurt by the Church in one way or another. They bring their kids to church to receive sacraments because they recognize that faith is important. But they have no interest in participating themselves. They tried it at one time in their lives and were unaffected by poor ministry or even hurt by it. Their own pastoral needs were not met.

In my early years of working in youth ministry, when I would present my youth program and sacramental requirements to parents, I could sense their hostility. They didn't want to do more paperwork. They didn't have time to volunteer. Every parish requirement for a sacrament meant one more obligation that they had to cram into their overpacked calendar. They also had little hope that the youth program was going to meet their children's basic pastoral needs. These parents truly had the right desires. They wanted meaningful relationships for their teenagers, and they wanted their own need for *support in their vocation as parents* heard by the parish leadership.

Parents are the people who express the most dissatisfaction with the state of youth ministry in the Church. True, they don't always understand or prioritize their children's need for catechesis, but I have *never* had a parent turn down the opportunity to have an additional adult mentor in his child's life.

Over the years, I have changed the conversation I have with parents. I began pursuing relationships with parents so that ministry for their teenager became a partnership. I dropped strict requirements in youth ministry and adopted flexibility so that the ministry didn't burden parents but supported and communicated with them.

As soon as I changed my approach with parents to a conversation about meeting pastoral needs, the parents almost immediately got on board with what I was proposing (more on this in chapter 7).

This doesn't mean that we abandon curriculum and prayer with young people; it means that we have to change the manner in which we communicate with parents to provide the right context for formation to take place.

Ministry Professionals Can Make Parents the Enemy

I recently spoke with a parent who had started a small-group Bible study with teens because her parish had no high school youth ministry. The pastor had given approval for the Bible study, and the handful of teens were delighted. The ministry wasn't large, but the small number of teens had their pastoral needs met in this environment, and they loved the little community that had formed.

Eventually, the pastor hired a youth minister for the parish. The youth minister launched a youth-group program and told the parent that he wanted the teens who were attending the Bible study to attend the youth group instead. The youth minister did not approve of the teens' meeting apart from the parish youth group (I think the youth minister felt threatened by the parent and her group). The youth minister communicated this to the parent, and the parent stopped meeting with the teens so as to avoid hostilities with the parish leadership. The teens didn't like the new youth program and eventually stopped going to it. As a result, none of the teens got their needs met.

I know this is not the norm for all parishes. Many parishes would love to have parents engaged and willing to lead Bible studies. I give this example to make an important point. When I speak with religious-education and youth-ministry leaders in the Church, they are all too ready to heap blame for the Catholic youth-ministry problem on parents. Ministry professionals blame parents for failing to practice the Faith in their home, for failing to catechize their children, and, therefore, for pushing their children one day to join the ranks of the "nones" by leaving the Catholic Church.

This blame may be fair, but only to a certain degree. If parents are to blame for failing to raise their children in the Faith, ministry leaders are also to blame for failing to engage and partner with parents who are willing to raise their children in the Faith. Ministry professionals are frequently responsible for increasing the division between parents and parish ministry, instead of partnering with parents to form young disciples.

Furthermore, some parish programs can even increase the cultural gap between the world of adults and that of young people. Some parishes in America have started faith-formation programs to catechize the parents of young people. Although well-intentioned, this can backfire by making family life suffer. Time taken out of parents' busy schedules is more time that parents are spending separated from their children. I'm not suggesting that parents should not pursue community and formation, but a parish must be mindful of what it is asking parents to do and whether it feeds the needs of families and parents or takes away from family life.

For example, I know of one parish that required parents to attend weekly classes on the Faith while their kids were having weekly classes in preparation for Confirmation. The classes were poorly taught, and many of the parents struggled to come up with weekly childcare for their other children. This resulted in resentment by parents rather than nourishing their pastoral needs.

I have even seen some parishes run a parent-formation program simultaneous with their youth program. This can send the message to families that teens should have their own space, separated from adults. Some parishes have youth Masses on Sunday and actively encourage teens to attend a separate Mass from their families. Again, I'm not suggesting that parishes shouldn't have liturgies that engage young people or that teens should not have a space in the parish where they feel welcome. But we have to be mindful of the message that we send to our teens and our parents in the Church—and it should never be a message of *division*.

The separation of teens from adults is not unique to the Church. It's a *cultural* problem. But the worst thing that the Church can do is feed into this problem by *dividing* young people from adults instead of *integrating* youth into the world of adults. This cannot be achieved if we make parents the enemy, or if our programs continue to separate adults and teens so that teens don't have adult example and mentorship.

CHAPTER 5

The Parish Problem:
Why Youth Groups Fail

I recently had lunch with a prominent Catholic author, and we discussed some of our future ministry projects. I told her I was writing a book about youth ministry and the challenges that parishes face.

She said: "I didn't like my parish youth group when I was growing up."

"Oh," I responded, "what didn't you like about it?"

"Everything. The games, the silliness.... The only thing I liked was the small-group discussion time. But that was usually too short to get into topics that were meaningful. I wish we had more time for those relationships to develop."

I can't tell you how many conversations I've had like this over the last several years. Whether it's parents, young adults who've grown up with a youth group, disengaged teens, or leaders in parishes, my experience has been that there is a growing consensus about the fruitlessness of youth groups in parishes. You can sum it up in five words: *youth groups are not working*.

Several years ago, I went to a youth-ministry development conference. During the conference, all the attendees were taken to a parish where we were able to observe an excellent, well-executed youth group.

The teens went to a Sunday-night liturgy that was very well done — respectful in the way it presented worship in the liturgy, while creating an environment where teens felt welcome and inviting full participation. After Mass, a team of adults served the teens dinner, and then the youth group started. There were several full-time youth ministers employed in the parish and an excellent team of adult volunteers. The presentation of the faith was dynamic and engaging, and I was impressed to see the teens participating. The team of adults had built a set for that evening to create an environment that matched the theme of the teaching. The parish's level of commitment to the teens was impressive.

As I stood in the back, observing the youth group, I thought one thing: *this would be a nightmare to duplicate*.

For this model to engage every teen in the parish, it needed a full-time youth minister (or several youth ministers); a large team of well-trained adults who regularly receive mentoring from parish leadership; teen recruitment strategies; a large budget to feed teens every week; a lot of work on weekly presentations; an excellent music ministry, environment, and sets; and a hospitality team trained to engage young people. Years later, one more thing became clear to me: none of these efforts were directed toward the most important part of youth ministry — meeting the basic needs of teens. These strategies presented an excellent program for teens, but none of these strategies engaged teens on the basic level of relationship.

One of the most common methods that parishes employ to meet teens' pastoral needs is the youth group. I have seen some youth groups and youth ministers do tremendous work in some parishes. There is no doubt that when a youth group is executed very well—with a large number of well-trained adults investing in the lives of a large number of teens—this model can make disciples. That being said, I think that the youth-group model presents many challenges for parishes that wish to be successful in discipling teens. There are inherent problems in the youth-group model that present obstacles for any parish. Moreover, there's a much more efficient and realistic way to meet the needs of teens in a parish.

The Problems with the Youth-Group Mentality

"We may live in a culture in which bigger has become synonymous with better," writes Mark DeVries, "but we serve a Lord who spoke of his kingdom in terms of a mustard seed, a widow's mite, and a single lost sheep. I love building a crowd. It makes me feel good. It makes me look good. And because of what building a crowd does for me, I have often mistaken short-term success for long-term effectiveness."[11] DeVries criticizes traditional youth ministry—the youth-group model—and essentially argues that we can be very successful at attracting teens to our programs, but this does not necessarily translate into forming disciples. He is critical of youth groups because he hasn't see any long-term results from them.

A youth group tries to create an entertaining or interactive presentation of the Faith for a large number of teenagers in one space. Yet successful youth ministry has little to do with the programs presented to teens and everything to do with the relationships that teens have with the people mentoring them.

---

[11] DeVries, *Family-Based Youth Ministry*, 29.

THE ART OF FORMING YOUNG DISCIPLES

Even when a youth group is executed well, there are inherent problems that affect the success of the ministry. Here are a few.

Group meetings engage few teens

Any time you give a lesson to a large number of teens, you are guaranteed not to connect with the majority of them. A freshman and a senior in high school are on totally different levels, and with only one teaching given each week, a youth minister can't possibly speak on the level of every teen in the room. Some teens need basic evangelization, and others want to go deeper. Some teens need a teaching on the importance of prayer, while others may be ready to dive into Ignatian spirituality. Large-group faith formation requires the youth minister to choose either a basic track or a deeper track, ensuring that he will miss the majority of his audience. Also, grouping all teens together for one catechetical lesson makes critical thinking difficult because the setting is too large for teens to engage in discussion and ask questions.

No teen wants a relationship
with every teen in the parish

Teens need relationships with their peers to hold them accountable to their Faith, but if the goal is to help teens connect and grow in deep friendships with a handful of their peers, it's counterproductive to have large groups of teens meeting in one space. Such an environment is the opposite of one that establishes trust and transparency.

Most people usually have only a handful of close friends. I'm much more likely to discuss the struggles of my life with a close friend over coffee than with thirty friends at a dinner party. Likewise, teens don't have a basic need to know every other teen in the parish.

Large-group youth programs hinder ministry

In today's culture, teens and their parents are overcommitted and too busy. There is no one day or time in the week when all teens in the parish are available to meet at the parish for a youth-group program. By scheduling youth ministry for one day of the week, parishes inhibit the growth of youth ministry by eliminating teens and adult volunteers who are not available that day. Good youth ministry provides flexibility so that every teen can participate.

Youth groups are generally superficial

There are times when I appreciate a good icebreaker, game, funny presentation, skit, or movie clip to pull me into a presentation. If this is presented to me every week, however, I get annoyed and irritated. As a youth minister, I've spent countless hours preparing sets and environments, setting up and breaking down the parish hall, preparing skits, searching through YouTube clips, and preparing and collecting materials for icebreakers. Even with a team of adult volunteers to assist me, the amount of work involved in creating an excellent youth-group presentation is staggering. Every hour spent preparing a presentation is one less hour spent in relationship with teens — and relationships are where basic needs get met.

Not only does creating excellent youth-group presentations make parish youth ministry high-maintenance, but there's also the problem of holding teens' attention for a ninety-minute presentation on a topic of the Faith. Keeping the teens stimulated and amused results in superficial presentations of the Faith.

Don't get me wrong: I'm not against having fun in youth ministry. But fun isn't always achieved in a youth-group setting. Many times, the presentations come across as silly (think about hand motions to worship songs). As a result, one of the most important virtues that youth culture values is lost: the virtue of authenticity. Teens are willing to dive into deeper questions of the Faith, but it's difficult to take them there after a silly skit or after a youth minister gets pied in the face.

Popular youth ministers are not the answer

I'm a very talented youth minister (on top of being very humble … and handsome). I know I can keep an audience engaged if I'm given the responsibility of giving a presentation to a large group. That comes with more than a decade of experience, a lot of education, and some natural talent and training mixed in. The problem is, if I succeed in giving a dynamic presentation to youth every week and then leave the parish, the ministry falls apart. Why? Because I would have built the entire ministry around my talents.

In many cases, effective large-group youth ministry depends on the gifts and talents of a particular youth minister. Only 12 percent of parishes currently pay a full-time youth minister, and the average burnout for a parish youth minister is around two years.[12] Given these statistics, if successful youth ministry depends on finding a dynamic youth minister, the Church is going to struggle to build sustainable youth ministry in parishes.

For more than two decades now, Catholic dioceses and organizations have been trying to address the Catholic youth-ministry problem by developing more-qualified youth ministers through degree programs and certification processes. Unfortunately, the

---

[12] Mark M. Gray, Mary L. Gautier, and Melissa A. Cidade, *The Changing Face of U.S. Catholic Parishes* (Washington, DC: National Association for Lay Ministry, 2011), 64.

turnover rate is so high in this field that even when a youth minister is well educated, he tends to leave a parish before making a lasting impact, and so the certification processes are largely ineffective in addressing the problem.

Don't get me wrong. I'm not recommending that lay ministers abandon ongoing formation or that parishes fire their youth ministers. What I have concluded, however, is that hiring a youth minister to fix a parish youth-ministry problem or developing certification processes is only a drop in the bucket. If the goal is to meet the pastoral needs of every teen in the parish, hiring a capable youth minister alone is not going to achieve this goal.

Youth groups can be quite expensive

Youth groups can be very expensive. They depend on a herd mentality to be successful. This means that a large number of teens have to come in order for the group to feel that it's something worth coming to.

How do you get teens to come to the parish every week? You have to make coming to church attractive. The church must feel like a place where a teen wants to be on a Sunday night. The problem with this is that parishes are some of the least welcoming and inviting places for teens. Think about where teens enjoy spending their time. They feel comfortable at home, sometimes at school, at the mall, or in coffee shops—pretty much everywhere except in a stale church hall. The Catholic parish is not the teens' turf.

So, how do parishes generally make the church environment more welcoming for teens? They throw money at the problem. If you do a weekly youth group, there's almost always food and beverages served (cheap pizza and soda). There might be a designated youth space, with games, electronics, and old, donated furniture.

Sometimes parishes will try to build a set or environment every week, to make the church space feel more fun or different for the youth group. All these things cost money—sometimes thousands of dollars in the parish budget. At best, these efforts make hanging out at the parish more tolerable for teens, but they rarely make the parish more comfortable than a coffee shop or the teens' homes. The result is a large amount of money sunk into costs that don't translate into making disciples.

Youth groups are largely obsolete

As I said earlier, I've seen some parish youth ministries have modest success with youth groups. I've met many youth ministers who are big advocates for them. I don't believe that you can entirely blame the youth group for the challenges that the Church faces with young people today. All that said, several years ago I took a step back and looked at the youth ministries I had built in parishes—youth groups that had varying degrees of success and required an enormous amount of my time and attention to be successful. I looked at what I was doing and thought, "There has got to be an easier way to do this."

I don't believe youth groups are bad.

I believe they're *inefficient*.

If the goal of youth ministry is to meet the pastoral needs of every teen in the parish, a youth group is not the easiest way to get there. I had a conversation with my pastor recently—a pastor who has been a FOCUS missionary and whose vision of ministry largely lines up with mine. He's a young man, a first-time pastor, and has a reputation for being a fantastic priest in my archdiocese. When I sat down with him to pitch my ideas for developing a youth ministry in our parish, he interrupted me and took the words right out of my mouth.

He said, "Youth groups are not working. They're becoming obsolete. We need to do something different."

I couldn't have said it better myself. I believe that in the next ten years the Catholic Church is going to see the youth-group model of ministry become *obsolete*. This is not to say that we won't see parishes utilizing youth groups. Catholic parishes tend to utilize models of ministry long after they've been determined to be ineffective. But I believe that the Church is headed for a consensus that the youth-group model of ministry is out of date. Something else is needed. Once that something else is established, youth groups will fall out of favor.

Religious-education-based ministries don't work

I have spent the entire chapter focusing on one model — the youth group — but there are other models: the youth-activities approach and classroom-based religious education. I'll briefly address these two models here.

Youth activities became popular over forty years ago as a method of youth ministry intended to get teens to participate in their parishes. They largely consist of a series of organized fun activities that teens attend at the parish — and that's basically it. That isn't youth ministry because there's no ministering involved. This approach doesn't make disciples because teens don't have any of their basic needs met. The model consists entirely of trying to get teens to participate in their parish. Although I believe that a parish youth ministry should be fun, making it exclusively about social gatherings quickly leaves teens disinterested.

Teens can have social gatherings anywhere. They don't need to come to church to have a social life (unless they're among the handful of teens who have no social life). Youth ministry has to be about a lot more than social gatherings. The youth-activities mentality is about getting teens to participate in their parish; it's not about making young people into lifelong disciples of Jesus Christ.

Even worse are the religious-education programs that parishes put in place for teenagers. These are sometimes called CCD (Confraternity of Christian Doctrine), PSR (Parish School of Religion), or Confirmation preparation programs. Regardless of what they're called, they're still the most common form of youth faith formation.

If the goal of youth ministry is to meet the pastoral needs of teens, then religious education *may be the worst approach to Catholic youth ministry in the Church's two-thousand-year history.*

In religious-education programs, parishes require teenagers to sit in a classroom with a volunteer catechist for two hours each week and receive systematic catechesis on Catholicism. I had a professor in college who said, "It's a mortal sin to bore someone with the gospel." If that's true, there are a lot of catechists who are going to Hell.

If you had a room full of youth-ministry experts tasked with developing an approach to meet a teen's basic needs, you would never hear the following proposed as a solution:

> I know how we can minister to teens! Let's stick teens in a classroom, because teenagers *love* school and want to spend more time there! We'll give a volunteer catechist one hour each week to teach them dogmas that are unrelated to their everyday life! The catechist will have little or no formation himself—in fact, we'll just take any volunteer we can get from the pew! And we'll give that catechist a poorly written textbook and throw him to the wolves! This will make our young people into disciples!

I've been to parishes all over the country. I've seen a lot of parishes that utilize this approach in their parish formation of teenagers. I've never seen a parish that can claim that this model has contributed to the development of even a single young person into a disciple of Jesus Christ. If anything, religious education is successful at driving teens away from the Church.

Torture is a serious sin — this madness needs to stop. Jesus was very clear about what would happen to trees that bear no fruit. He said that those trees would be cut down and thrown into the fire (Matt. 7:19).

Today, parishes face all kinds of challenges when it comes to making teens into lifelong disciples. The models of the past are not working. There are too many flaws and problems with the typical approaches that parishes employ to engage teens. Something different is needed. Unfortunately for the Church, the challenges don't stop there. It's not just the parish that is struggling to meet the needs of young people.

CHAPTER 6

The Catholic School Problem: It's a Train Wreck

I'll never forget an experience I had in high school. I was on the track and field team and part of the "jumpers" — the group that trained to do long jump, triple jump, and high jump. Although the girls' track and field team and the boys' team were separate with different coaches, the boys' and the girls' jumpers would practice together with the same jumper coaches.

The boys on this team were all too eager to work side by side with the girls. When the girls weren't listening, the conversation almost always turned to comments about which girl was "hottest," and the guys regularly made inappropriate, sexual comments about the girls. They encouraged one another to "hook up" with them. Guys even made bets about whether they could get particular girls into bed.

One day, one of the male coaches overheard the guys on the team talking in this manner about one of the girls. He didn't put a stop to the discussion. He didn't correct or discipline the boys. Instead, *he joined the discussion*, making comments about the girl's body and encouraging the boys in their wager.

As a young, impressionable freshman in high school, I didn't fully understand the gravity of what I was witnessing. I just thought this was how boys and men acted. After all, such conversations were commonplace in the hallways of the high school. Why wouldn't a coach join in on the joking around? It wasn't until later in my life that I realized just how terrible a witness this was for me and how scandalous and troublesome it was that a coach was acting in this manner. To make matters worse, this coach was a math teacher in the school … and it was a *Catholic school*.

The Terrifying Reality of Catholic Education

Catholic education represents the single biggest investment in youth ministry in the Catholic Church. Every diocese pours millions of dollars into Catholic education, not to mention all the time and talent that's invested as well. A Catholic school has the chance to work with students for the better part of their week, and even in their extracurricular activities, to form their intellect and values. Apart from parents, a Catholic school has the greatest opportunity to impact the lives and direction of young persons.

This is a difficult subject to address in a general manner, because Catholic schools have different administrations, faculty, demographics, and other factors. I know of some tremendous Catholic schools, at primary, secondary, and higher-education levels, that do an excellent job of both educating and forming young people into disciples of Jesus Christ. I also know many outstanding and inspiring teachers and have many friends who work in Catholic education.

But there are also many Catholic schools that are Catholic in name only. I attended Catholic schools from kindergarten through college. My wife attended Catholic schools for most of her life, as did my sister and brother-in-law and many of my friends. Most of us had similar experiences. Here are some of the things that I commonly hear from alumni of Catholic schools:

- The vast majority of our classmates are no longer practicing Catholicism.
- Bullying and cliques were commonplace.
- The religion teachers knew little or no theology and were not equipped to teach even the most basic dogmatic teachings.
- Many of the teachers demonstrated little understanding of Catholicism, and many were not practicing Catholics.
- Administrators were lacking in their witness of Catholic values to the students.
- The student subculture within the school was saturated with drug and alcohol abuse and promiscuity.
- There were liturgies filled with all kinds of abuses — including liturgical dance, skits during the Mass, and other gimmicks to try to get kids more involved in the Mass.
- Catholic teaching focused primarily on service to others and moral teaching, which was basically a list of the rules we were supposed to follow in our lives.

This doesn't even begin to consider issues with the majority of Catholic university campuses, where the problems can be much, much worse.

These experiences are not limited to my family and friends. A Catholic secondary school in the state of Washington made national headlines when it fired a vice principal because he married his gay partner. The school administration and the student body knew that the vice principal was gay and was living with his partner. It was public knowledge. They fired him only when he married his partner. This is a scandal for many reasons — not the least of which is that the vice principal should never have been hired in the first place.[13]

According to another news story, a Catholic diocese fired a teacher for publicly acknowledging that she was actively pursuing in vitro fertilization (a violation of Catholic bioethics teaching and teachings on the dignity of human life). The Catholic-school principal said that he did not know that in vitro fertilization was against Church teaching.[14]

There is a crisis in Catholic education — many of our schools do not take seriously the task of forming disciples or simply do not know how to do so.

The Changing Culture of Catholic Education

Of course, there are a good number of people who don't want to admit that Catholic education is failing. After all, there is a huge investment in it. Several decades ago, every Catholic family sent their children to Catholic schools. The attitude of families was that it was the school's responsibility to form young persons in the Faith (which has contributed to the problem of parents failing to raise their children in the Faith). With the rise of tuition and expenses in Catholic schools and the growth

---

[13] Levi Pulkkinen, "Eastside Catholic Vice Principal Ousted after Gay Marriage Drops Lawsuit," *SeattlePI*, November 28, 2014, http://www.seattlepi.com/local/article/Vice-principal-ousted-for-Eastside-Catholic-after-5919802.php.

[14] Peter Jesserer Smith, "Diocese to Lose $2 Million in Teacher's IVF Lawsuit," *National Catholic Register*, December 27, 2014, http://www.ncregister.com/daily-news/diocese-to-lose-2-million-in-teachers-ivf-lawsuit.

of public education (which is paid for by taxes), more and more Catholics sought alternatives to Catholic schools.

I've met many older pastors who hold to the idea that youth ministry in their parish consists of the Catholic school, and that is all they offer. This is a very outdated mind-set. Fewer Catholic families send their children to Catholic schools than ever before.

In the 1950s and 1960s, Catholic schools had the luxury of having very little overhead expense. Nuns and priests didn't need to be paid much to work. But with the decline in vocations and the massive number of Catholic schools, the schools had to turn to lay teachers to keep themselves staffed. This meant an increase in tuition in order to pay lay teachers a living wage (something that many Catholic schools still struggle to do). Furthermore, very few lay teachers had formal philosophical or theological training. There soon became little to differentiate Catholic-school education from public-school education. If there is no difference in the quality or type of education, people are not going to pay for something they can get for free.

To keep their doors open, Catholic schools — which had previously been very affordable — had to increase tuition greatly. Many Catholic schools tried to provide more value by focusing almost entirely on "academic excellence."

Don't get me wrong. Academic excellence should be the mark of every Catholic school. But when it becomes the sole focus and primary marketable asset of the education, the school fails to attract a student-body that reflects the Catholic values necessary to create a Catholic subculture.

Many Catholic schools are still subsidized by local parishes, leaving those parishes with insufficient funds for ministry to Catholic youth outside of Catholic schools. This, too, is unhealthy because the majority of Catholic young people do not attend Catholic schools (likely because their families cannot afford it). There's nothing less Catholic than a dichotomy in which only the wealthy youth are "ministered" to.

Many Catholic schools wound up courting affluent families that were not interested in forming disciples; they wanted "successful children." These families may be attracted to the "academic excellence" of Catholic education but not necessarily to Catholic formation. Students who are under high pressure to perform tend to be more susceptible to drugs, alcohol, promiscuity, depression, and suicide. Affluence can become a recipe for a student environment that is anything but Catholic.

As a youth minister, I always said I was more interested in what was happening in the hallways at school than in what was happening in the classrooms. A Catholic school can have the best teaching methods, the best Catholic teachers, and the best curriculum, but without a student body focused on living their Faith (because they come from families that reinforce faith), the student subculture in the school will never be truly Catholic.

More and more faithful Catholic families are turning to homeschooling. Many of these families (because they are open to life and faithfully living out Catholic teaching) have many children, and putting them all through Catholic schools is not affordable. Ironically, many homeschooled youths end up better educated and more mature in their Faith because they have adult guidance daily and their education is individualized to meet their needs.

Catholic schools are missing out on these families. These are exactly the young people who can change the environment of the Catholic school to create a true, Catholic subculture.

The Lack of Orthodoxy in Catholic Schools

There's another layer to the problems in Catholic education: lack of orthodoxy. *Orthodoxy* means "right teaching." When we say that a teaching is orthodox, we mean that it reflects the consistent teachings of our Catholic Tradition and the authority of our bishops.

After Vatican II, there was a significant rebellion within the Catholic Church. Many priests, nuns, religious, and even some bishops dissented from the traditional teachings of the Church. They were dissatisfied that the Church had not changed several doctrines — largely doctrines on sexuality. Dissenters found a safe haven in seminaries and Catholic universities — the two major institutions of Catholic higher education.

In 1967, Fr. Theodore Hesburgh, CSC, invited leaders from Catholic universities in America to the Land O' Lakes Conference. Much can be written about the impact of this conference, but the long and short of it is that these leaders signed a statement that declared that their Catholic universities were separate from Church hierarchy. They did not want their universities to be accountable to the local bishop or to the Church hierarchy. By 1972, virtually every Catholic university in America had taken similar steps. This allowed Catholic universities to become institutions for "religious dialogue" and "free thought," which meant that they became a safe haven for Church dissenters. By the mid-1970s, it was virtually impossible to receive an orthodox Catholic theology education in America.

The effect of this conference on the Catholic identity of primary and secondary Catholic schools was catastrophic. With the majority of lay teachers being educated at these universities, it became difficult to find teachers who were capable of teaching and witnessing the "right teachings" of the Catholic Church.

Catholic education went through a crisis of faith for several decades and even still feels the effects of this great Catholic dissent.

Today, sadly, the majority of Catholic universities remain Catholic in name only. Georgetown University—a once proud Jesuit university—recently invited the president of Planned Parenthood to give a keynote address on its campus. Many Catholic universities still don't offer a theology degree but instead offer "religious studies"—incorporating new-age spirituality, Buddhism, and many other religions into their curriculum. Pro-choice Catholic politicians—many of whom are products of these Catholic universities—are regularly invited to give addresses on Catholic campuses. Some Catholic campuses are even teaching liberation theology, a combination of socialism and theology that was popularized in South America and was condemned by the Congregation for the Doctrine of the Faith. The majority of Catholic universities in America still have anemic campus ministries.

The lack of fidelity in Catholic universities has had a trickle-down effect into primary and secondary Catholic education. With fewer and fewer priests and nuns teaching in classrooms, Catholic schools had to pull teachers from somewhere. This meant that many students who had been formed in dissenting Catholic-university environments became teachers in primary and secondary Catholic schools.

This lack of orthodoxy, more than anything else, has contributed to the train wreck that is Catholic education.

Hope for Catholic Schools

Reform in Catholic education has been occurring, but it will be several more decades before we see a full, positive reform. Franciscan University of Steubenville, Benedictine College in

Kansas, and Ave Maria University in Florida (to name a few) are dynamic Catholic universities that are orthodox and incorporate Catholic identity into every facet of their schools. The Cardinal Newman Society publishes a list of Catholic universities whose theology faculty take an oath of fidelity to the teachings of the Church and to their local bishop. The list is growing, as is high-quality campus ministry at both Catholic and state colleges, promoted by organizations such as FOCUS.

I am an alumnus of Franciscan University of Steubenville. I was blown away by my experience of formation and education on the campus. The chapel for daily Mass was full three times a day. So was the Perpetual Adoration Chapel. In fact, to avoid the crowds at the campus's Adoration Chapel, many students attended Eucharistic Adoration off campus or went to Blessed Sacrament chapels in their dorms. Missionary work—in town, domestic, and foreign—was a regular part of many of the students' lives.

Students' pastoral needs were met through a variety of ministries—most notably the household system. Developed by Fr. Michael Scanlon, TOR, the "household system" was a reformed fraternity/sorority structure in which students shared their lives communally with one another. These communities were committed to patron saints, apostolates, accountability, virtue, and prayer.

What Catholic Education Should Look Like

The first time I visited Franciscan University, I noticed that there were no false appearances on the campus. Students lived their Faith and supported one another. Each faculty and staff member was hired with the intention of putting Catholic witnesses in front of the students. Even maintenance workers were regulars at daily Mass on campus. Prayer was a way of life, and older students — who had matured in their Christian witness as a result of their environment — supported younger students.

Disciples make disciples. We cannot expect to form youth into lifelong disciples of Jesus Christ unless we put them into relationships with people who are already disciples. It is not enough for a school to hire a few good religion teachers or a campus minister, or to have a few priests teaching on campus. Every person a student encounters on school property must be actively trying to be a Christian witness. When a student is saturated in Catholicism as a lived experience, he cannot help but be formed by those experiences.

More and more faithful Catholic universities are popping up around the country, and it is having a trickle-down effect in the worlds of secondary and primary education. Because many secondary and primary schools are run directly by dioceses (and therefore are under the care of the local bishop), making dramatic changes in Catholic schools is not in principle difficult. There is still hope for this model and signs of life within these schools.

What Catholic Education Can Look Like

I would never suggest that the Catholic Church abandon her efforts in education. There's too much history and too much potential for evangelization in Catholic schools. Rather, I want Catholic education to reclaim its identity.

Catholic education has always been set apart in its approach to formation. It is supposed to make virtues, prayer, art, music, liberal arts, service, and physical activity vital components of the education process. True Catholic education should form the worldview of a young mind.

It isn't simply about having a religion class, service hours, or liturgies available for children. Catholicism can and should be taught in every subject. For example, Church history can be taught within history classes. I never knew that the French Revolution was a direct attack on Catholicism until I studied it in a truly Catholic college. I didn't even know what Freemasonry was. In junior high in a Catholic school, I had been taught that the French Revolution was a good thing. That's a result of the school's failure to integrate Catholicism into every class.

Catholics have long been creating influential works in literature, art, and music. Catholicism has a long history of scientific discovery, which can be introduced in the study of science. Philosophy should be a part of all Catholic education. Students should come out of a Catholic school with the ability to think and to reason. This is necessary for a virtuous person.

Many Catholic schools talk about forming the whole person, but few actually do it, although the numbers of those that do so are increasing. In Denver, where I live, a poor Catholic school was on the brink of closure. The pastor fought hard to keep the school open and hired a principal to implement a classical curriculum for the school, focusing on the great literary works of different eras, the study of languages and philosophy, and integration of the arts into daily life. The pastor worked hard to provide students with financial aid so that no one would be turned away and they could keep the school open. The principal hired new, young teachers who actively lived their Faith and were capable of teaching a classical education. The doors of the school stayed open, and the school soon added a Montessori preschool.

Word spread in the Catholic community, and strong Catholic families began recruiting for the school. Soon many of the local homeschooling families put some of their children in the school.

In a few short years, the student body more than tripled, and the school had a waiting list for admission. Now this school, once on the verge of closing, is doing a capital campaign so it can expand. The Catholic community of families within the school is amazing, and the parish is reaping benefits, too.

I had the opportunity to run a few youth-ministry activities in its junior high. I've never been more impressed with the quality of young disciples. There were no cliques (in fact, most of the students were comfortable with students of all ages). There was no drama. The teachers were genuinely interested in the lives of their students, and they all appeared to be cut from the same cloth. The students sought out the Lord in their young prayer lives. They were mature, articulate, and virtuous. I spent time with students outside the classroom and even in some of their homes. They were the same kids in each of those environments. Not all of this can be attributed to the school. After all, the school was actively trying to recruit good Catholic families. But this was a Catholic school that I can honestly say forms young disciples.

PART 3

The Twofold Solution

CHAPTER 7

Small-Group Discipleship

In the previous chapters, I demonstrated that Catholic youth ministry is failing to meet the basic pastoral needs of young people. There are layers to the problem — the culture, the family, obsolete parish-ministry approaches, and many obstacles within Catholic education.

Now let us consider some of the elements that I believe make good youth ministry work.

The Huge Impact of a Small Group

The tailor Jan Tyranowski lived in Poland during the 1930s. He was a common layman who had a great love for Christ and the Catholic Church. As a young man, he committed his life to Christ when he heard a priest say, "It's not difficult to become a saint." Tyranowski resolved to read spiritual classics and soon developed a great devotion to the spiritual works of St. John of the Cross. Jan Tyranowski is currently being considered for canonization.

I believe that this humble Polish tailor — a man who was simply devoted to living a saintly life — may have had one of the greatest impacts on the world in the twentieth century. In 1939, the Nazis invaded Poland and began removing priests from parishes because they felt threatened by the priests' influence over their congregations. The Nazis feared that the Catholic Church and the priests might lead an uprising against the Nazis in heavily Catholic Poland. In particular, the Nazis targeted priests in youth programs, not wanting the priests to interfere with their attempted indoctrination of Polish young people.

As a result of the shortage of priests, some parishes turned to laypersons to help form young people. At St. Stanislaus Kostka parish, Tyranowski was seen as a prayerful man, so he was asked to work with high-school-aged boys in the parish.

Tyranowski started a youth ministry he called "The Living Rosary," selecting five older boys to mentor in the Faith. Through his instruction, these five young men became very committed to living a disciplined life and devoted to a deep mysticism—especially the study and practice of St. John of the Cross's spirituality. Tyranowski met with these boys every week and mentored them in their lives and in the Faith. He instructed each of those young men to find twelve younger boys to meet with weekly. Altogether, in this small-group-based Living Rosary, there were sixty-five boys. Ten of them became priests.

The first of the ten to be ordained was a young man named Karol Wojtyla—who went on to become Pope St. John Paul II. Later, when reflecting on his life, Wojtyla said, "Tyranowski's influence was instrumental for me. If it were not for Jan Tyranowski, I would not have become a priest." Karol Wojtyla did his doctoral dissertation on the spiritual works of St. John of the Cross.

A simple Polish tailor who lived a holy life changed the entire course of human history by mentoring five young men.[15]

---

[15] George Weigel, *Witness to Hope: The Biography of Pope John Paul II* (New York: Cliff Street Books, 1999), 58–62.

The "Sermon on the Mount" Mentality

In my introduction, I mentioned that I had an epiphany while lunching with a friend. I realized that in our existing forms of youth ministry, there is no way to meet every teen's basic pastoral needs.

The biggest problem I see in ministry today is that we have a "Sermon on the Mount" mentality. In His Sermon on the Mount, Jesus gave a long series of teachings (Matt. 5–7) to a great number of people. Scripture doesn't say that the people who heard that sermon went on to become His most faithful disciples. The content of the Sermon on the Mount was important — so important that it made it into Matthew's Gospel, but, so far as we know, it didn't form its listeners into lifelong disciples.

Jesus had twelve apostles. Those twelve lived with Him and were mentored by Him for three years. Those twelve carried the gospel all over the world. Those twelve were His biggest success story. Jesus' large-group ministry didn't have the biggest impact on the world; His small-group ministry changed the world.

As I mentioned in my introduction, several years ago I developed what I thought was a very successful youth-ministry program. Lots of teens participated in our weekly youth group and other events we put together — Bible studies, youth camps, service trips, conferences, retreats, youth liturgies, and so forth. I went to and even began speaking at national training conferences on youth ministry. At these conferences, I began to notice that virtually all the training and all the featured resources were based on large gatherings of youth.

I had already begun to question whether what I was doing in my parish youth ministry was effective. I questioned whether any of my education had taught me the best practices. I realized I might have to make a drastic change in approach if I were going to meet the pastoral needs of teens.

What if, instead of thinking of all the youth in the parish as one large group, I thought about them as a series of small groups?

What if I abandoned the youth-group concept and other programmed concepts in favor of doing ministry the way Jesus did it?

What if I stopped giving Sermons on the Mount and instead spent my efforts in youth ministry developing a system of discipleship—one in which I invested my time in a handful of teenagers and other adult mentors instead of trying to stretch myself to meet the needs of every young person?

Youth Ministry That Works

In 2011, I decided to experiment with youth ministry at my parish. That fall, I had asked a few of my adult volunteers each to select a small group of teens who were involved in the youth group and begin weekly small groups with them to mentor them more deeply in the Faith. Those small groups met in the homes of the teens or in coffee shops, where they would dig into the Bible and talk about prayer (we used the first versions of the YDisciple resources to get the group discussions started). Three small groups (involving twenty teens) were launched that semester.

I continued to offer the weekly youth group and all the programs I had previously been doing in the parish, but within weeks, my youth-group attendance dropped off dramatically. Virtually all the teens who were involved in weekly small groups stopped attending youth group.

When I ran into one of the high school seniors who had previously been very involved in the youth group but had stopped attending, I asked her why I never saw her at youth group anymore.

She told me, "I have my small group of girls—I love it. Honestly, I just don't feel like I need the youth group anymore. I'm learning so much more in this small group, and my girlfriends are holding me accountable."

Bingo!

This girl made clear to me that her pastoral needs were being met in this small group. Years later, I looked her up. She's still practicing her Faith (she's a daily Mass attendee) and is married to a great Catholic man. They are expecting their first child. She was very involved in her college campus ministry. She became a lifelong disciple.

By the end of that semester, I had virtually stopped doing the youth group altogether. We were doing youth group only once a month (as a way to build community between the small groups), and most of the teens who had been coming to the youth group had joined newly formed small groups that were led by adult core team members.

Within one year, I went from having three small groups of teens to having twelve small groups. I went from having a weekly youth group with 60 teens participating to having 120 teens discipled in small groups that met throughout the week (in many locations). The youth ministry doubled in size in a year's time, but what was more important was that discipleship was happening and pastoral needs were being met.

I loved small-group discipleship because I was no longer spending my time planning silly activities and dynamic presentations for the youth group. I was free to spend my time mentoring the handful of teens I was passionate about and mentoring adults who were leading the small groups.

The teens loved the small groups because the attention they received was individualized and the small groups were meeting on their own turf (homes, coffee shops, their school). They developed close friendships and found that they were listened to and understood by their group leader. They found a sense of belonging; they could be transparent about what was going on in their lives; and they could get their questions about the Faith answered.

The core team of adult volunteers loved the small groups because they could focus all their attention on the same handful of teenagers every week, and they could see a real difference in the teens they were working with over the course of several years. They also got to meet with the teens when *their* schedule allowed for it, rather than having to give up their Sunday nights to assist at the mediocre youth group. This made it much easier to recruit more adults into the ministry.

Parents loved the small groups because they saw how small-group discipleship was meeting the basic needs of their teens. Many of them were more than willing to open their homes and host the small groups for dinner. This presented the opportunity to start to evangelize the entire family, because the simple gesture of doing ministry within the home presented the example of discipleship to the parents. The structure of the small groups also provided more flexibility, which accommodated the busy schedules of parents.

The pastor loved the small groups because the youth ministry was growing. Even more, he knew that if the youth minister eventually resigned and moved on to another opportunity, his youth ministry wouldn't fall apart. The youth ministry was built around the adult volunteers, not around the gifts and talents of one youth minister.

The structure worked. Making a simple adjustment to the way I did ministry — by developing a structure of ministry focused on meeting every teen's pastoral needs — changed the entire culture of youth ministry in my parish.

Shifting to Small-Group Discipleship

I've had the opportunity to offer workshops on small-group discipleship over the past several years. When I present to pastors, parents, or even young people, I almost always get an immediate, positive response. One of the hardest audiences to convince is youth ministers. Many are set in their ways and don't want to make dramatic adjustments to the way they do ministry.

One youth minister challenged me by saying, "We break into small groups for thirty minutes every week in the youth group." I'm sorry, but this is not discipleship. There's an enormous difference between small-group facilitation, whose purpose is to catechize, and small-group discipleship, whose purpose is to mentor and meet pastoral needs. I can't develop relationships with teens and dig into their lives if I have only thirty minutes with them each week.

What's more, many times in such youth groups, the small groups have different leaders and different teens each week. Discipleship requires intentional and consistent relationships. A mentor must be invested in the same group of young people for a long period in order to have a real impact.

Think about the way Jan Tyranowski did ministry. He focused virtually all his attention on five boys (who mentored twelve boys each). He poured his life into them, and they learned from his example. He was their rabbi. This simple ministry changed the world. Discipleship, by definition, requires a deliberate, cultivated relationship between a rabbi and a few disciples. Simply breaking into small groups doesn't accomplish this vital relationship. The relationships have to be cultivated, and they have to meet for more than thirty minutes in a large-group setting.

Another youth minister didn't think she could fit this model of ministry in with everything else she was doing. I asked about the ministry in her parish, and she told me that they did six retreats a year, sacramental preparation, weekly youth group, a weekly youth Mass, two service projects, a mission trip, and many other activities. I told her to stop doing all of that. I don't have anything against all that "stuff." Most of it has a great impact on teens. But I have come to believe that small-group discipleship is absolutely vital in order for youth ministry to succeed. If teens' pastoral needs aren't met, and they don't have a rabbi in their life, none of that other stuff will make up for missing that vital component of ministry. If their pastoral needs are being met, all that other stuff will become a great supplemental ministry that will build up and support discipleship.

We have to change how we do ministry. We can't keep using the same failed paradigms. Time and time again, I've spoken with young adults who are no longer practicing their Faith. I find that they grew up in a youth group or went to a Catholic school and didn't have their pastoral needs met. In every instance, I've asked the same question: "How would you like it if you could simply meet with me or another adult once a week in a coffee shop with a small group of your friends and could spend time digging into the questions that you have about God, sex, relationships, religion, and such, and you could get these questions answered?"

In every instance, these young adults tell me that that's exactly what they're looking for. They have tons of questions about religion and the Faith, and they want the Church to answer those questions. Discipleship is not complicated, but we need to stop wasting our time on ministry efforts that aren't yielding fruit.

The first step is simple — follow the example of Jan Tyranowski. Find some holy men and women in your parish and have them draw a handful of teenagers into their lives for weekly mentoring. Simplify the ministry approach and focus on what is most effective. Think small, in order to grow big. Raise up saints (like Pope St. John Paul II) and change the world.

CHAPTER 8

Parent-Focused Youth Outreach

One of the questions I often get is "How do we go about starting a small-group ministry?" I believe the most effective way is to start one small group at a time, with the help of parents.

As part of an experiment for a parish I was consulting with, I asked the pastor to give me the names of two parents who had a teenager and who practiced the Faith in their home. I invited those parents out for coffee. We spoke about their son and his needs. We discussed how a small group with a mentor would be a tremendous benefit for his faith development. We agreed that, in order for him to get fully invested in a small group, it would need to consist of his close friends. It didn't take long for these parents to get excited about the prospect of having a weekly small group for their son.

I knew that if I had his parents on board, I could get the teenager to participate. After all, parents largely control the schedules of their teenagers, and their son didn't drive yet, so he was reliant on his parents to take him places. The parents asked me, "How are you going to start this group?" I replied, "I'm not going to start it. You're going to start it. You're going to be my lead couple for this group." The parents didn't understand my response.

I explained to them that I didn't know their son's friends, and I wouldn't have any credibility with the parents of their son's friends. But they could easily identify all their son's friends and invite their parents over for coffee. At a coffee meeting with all the parents, I could give a short presentation and get everyone on board with the purpose and scheduling of the group. I also asked the parents to help me identify a great adult mentor for their son and his friends and told them I would approach that mentor and train him to work with the boys.

I *empowered the parents* to do the recruiting for the small group and to help me identify an adult mentor for their teenager.

The parents did the legwork—I simply provided them the support they needed to get a small group going.

It wasn't long before we had the small group off the ground, and I had done it by mobilizing a small army of concerned parents.

How do I start small-group youth ministry?

By *evangelization and outreach through parents*.

Why is this effective?

Because no one is more concerned about meeting the pastoral needs of young persons than their parents.

Parents Are the Solution

I've spoken with many people in the Church who understand that working with parents is one of the biggest challenges we face in youth ministry. Many parents have become disengaged from the Church for one reason or another, and most grew up in a generation that received both poor pastoral care and poor catechesis. As a result, parents tend to lack the tools and knowledge necessary to become spiritual leaders of their own families. Even if they have the tools, they don't always have the confidence to put their knowledge of the Faith to good use.

Over the past several years, I've heard many in the Church speak about the need to engage and empower parents as the primary catechists of their own teens. More and more, we are hearing about the need for family-based ministry. Yet I've seen a lack of vision in parent ministries. Very few parishes have launched a parent ministry as part of their youth ministry (outside of mandated parent catechesis nights as part of sacramental formation). Even fewer are running *successful* parent ministries.

Several years ago, I inherited a sacramental preparation program that included a parent catechesis element. Once a month, parents were required to attend a catechetical presentation on Sunday afternoons if they wanted their children to be approved for sacramental preparation. The presentations were boring, and the day or time was unfortunate (parents wanted to be watching football or spending time with their families on Sunday).

I agreed with the parish's identification of the problem — the parents in this parish were disengaged and poorly catechized. But I disagreed with their solution.

I had a good friend who was required to attend one of my parent catechesis sessions because she was the sponsor of a Confirmation candidate. I knew the sessions were brutal, but I was just trying to get through the year so I could make some changes in the following year. After the session, I asked her, "How was it?" She responded, "You really need to serve alcohol at these things." (That isn't a bad idea.)

Some parents may be poorly catechized, and some may be disengaged. The solution is not to trap them in a room together and bore them with the gospel. I don't think the solution is parent catechesis programs. If teens are overcommitted, parents are even more so: they're burned out. They have commitments every night of the week. They have stress at home and at work. Many parents have struggles with their kids and in their marriages. Being an adult and a parent in today's world is exceptionally challenging. The last thing parents want is to have to attend another commitment or to listen to a speaker articulate the dogmas of the Faith. They have pastoral needs as well, and those needs are not being met in traditional parent ministries.

Engaging Parents within Their Vocation

In the first chapter, I briefly discussed the five thresholds of conversion as introduced in the book *Forming Intentional Disciples*. The first two thresholds are *initial trust* and *spiritual curiosity*. Parents who were coming to my parent ministries had not crossed either of those thresholds. They were completely closed off, and the ministry we put into place did nothing to help them cross those thresholds. Our intentions were good, but simply attempting to catechize such adults won't work.

When I empower one lead couple to recruit a small group for their own teen, something amazing happens. Often, some of the parents are not practicing Catholics, or they've become disengaged from their Faith in one way or another. But regardless of where the parents are on their faith journey, they all have one thing in common: *they are deeply concerned about meeting their children's basic pastoral needs*.

I quickly discovered that the fastest way to help parents cross the first two thresholds is to speak to them not about the Faith but about their kids. I found that parents came alive in that discussion and immediately became engaged when they discovered that I understood the challenges of raising a teenager in today's world and that I was looking to provide them with help and support. This immediately opened up our discussions into the challenges that each of them faces and how small-group disciple-ship would assist them in meeting their children's pastoral needs.

This is encouraging news!

Parents may be disengaged from the Faith, but they have not abandoned their primary vocation! They understand that their vocation is to love their children, and they take that responsibility very seriously. And I know that I can help the parents to become re-engaged in their Faith by keeping them informed about what we are discussing in the small group. I know that the shortest path to conversion in parents' hearts is through their relationship with their teenagers.

I have trained the mentors of the small groups to connect with parents each week—whether by e-mail or some other way. This keeps parents actively engaged in what the teens are discussing in the group and keeps open lines of communication between parents and the youth ministry in the parish. In addition, parents are invited to host small groups in their homes—creating an opportunity for the group leader to deepen his relationship with parents. The small group becomes a partnership between parish youth ministry and parents to provide basic pastoral care for their youth.

Youth Outreach through Parents

When I had gotten the first small group off the ground, I asked the original lead parents to name another couple in the parish who would like me to start this process with them and their teenager. Immediately, I had parents I could contact to start a second small group.

Do the math: if there are 8 teens in every small group and you start 2 small groups with freshmen every year, you will have 64 teenagers engaged in high school youth ministry by the time the first two groups finish their senior year. That's 128 parents engaged in ministry by the time all these small groups have gotten off the ground. That's not just 64 teens participating in high school youth ministry. It's 64 teens actively and intentionally discipled by mentors within their small groups. Those 64 teens will have their basic needs met.

You just have to start two small groups each year; and the easiest way to do it is by empowering parents.

Also, consider this: there are many teens who will never come to a parish youth group or program. There are many teens who are on the fringes and will never receive an invitation to participate in your church. Parents have the most access to these teens. By engaging friends of their teens, parents may draw into the group some of those teens on the fringes. They can even reach out to teens who are in other parishes, or maybe even teens of other faiths. They can reach out to teens who are not practicing any faith. Meeting pastoral needs is something everyone wants; and every teen in the world has some level of curiosity about religion and faith. What better way to reach out to these teens than to mobilize an army of concerned parents to assemble small groups that invite teens on the fringes to participate?

I found that large-group youth activities (for the purposes of larger parish fellowship) were easier to execute once I had several small groups going well. All I had to do was tell my small-group mentors what we were going to do, and they would show up with their groups. It was an instant youth group. Teens were more willing to engage in activities at the parish (service, prayer, or fun) when they knew that their friends were coming.

I found that parents became very interested in having their own small groups when they saw how discipleship was changing their teenagers and meeting their pastoral needs. This opened up a whole new area of ministry, because true parent ministry was now possible.

This model has been highly effective for me over the last several years. It meets the pastoral needs of teens; it engages and empowers parents to assist in the discipleship of their teenagers; it is easy to grow; and it's a fraction of the work that my years of youth groups required of me.

A Practical Strategy

Here is a summary of a practical strategy to meet the pastoral needs of the teens in a parish and community.

1. With the help of your pastor, identify one set of parents—your first lead couple—who are serious disciples. Meet with that couple to discuss small groups.
2. With the help of that lead couple, identify and recruit two mentors for the first small group of five to eight teenagers.
3. Have the lead couple identify which of their teenager's friends to invite to participate in the small group. Have the couple invite the parents of each of those teenagers for coffee.
4. Get all the parents on board with the vision and purpose of the group. Set a time and location for the first meeting, and then begin.
5. Once the first small group is off and running, ask your lead couple to name another couple to start a second group.

It's simple. The tasks of the youth minister then become facilitation of the process, engagement of the parents, and mentoring the mentors of the small groups. Anything else done in youth ministry — retreats, mission trips, service projects, youth-group gatherings — supplements the discipleship that happens in the small groups.

When parents are engaged in this manner, outreach can grow exponentially. More importantly, parents are re-engaged in the process of forming their teenagers into disciples of Jesus Christ.

CHAPTER 9

The Recipe for Success

I firmly believe that for any youth ministry to be successful, there must be a vision in place to have every teen in a parish have an identifiable mentor and several friends who can hold each other accountable for growing in the Faith. I also believe that parents *must* be engaged in the process of discipleship with their children.

If a parish truly understands the Catholic youth-ministry problem, a variety of solutions can be put into place. My method of developing discipleship may be different from the strategies of other parishes, and both can be successful. The most important concept to understand is that all ministry has to meet the pastoral needs of the people to whom it ministers.

Strategies, Pitfalls, and Obstacles

Over the past several years, I have worked in a variety of settings to help youth ministries make the shift to small-group discipleship. I have helped parishes transition from a youth-group structure to a small-group structure. I have helped a small parish build a small-group youth ministry from scratch with volunteers. I have run my own small group in a Catholic-school environment and assisted the school's campus ministry in its development of a small-group structure. There are several obstacles I have encountered time and time again that are important to overcome when setting up these types of ministries. Here are a few key lessons I have learned about developing small-group ministry.

Start small, grow big

If you've ever been whitewater rafting, you will know that rafts never go down a rapid at the same time. If they did, they might collide with one another and flip each other over. Rafts are sent down a rapid one at a time.

When I started small-group youth ministry, I was still thinking programmatically. I wanted to have ten small groups with two leaders in each group. So I recruited twenty adults (which was a difficult task). I had a training day; we planned for launch; and we assigned teens to groups with the leaders.

The plan failed miserably.

It's not possible to program something that's supposed to happen organically. When I focus on starting one small group at a time and give the attention necessary to the leaders, to forming the dynamic of the group, and to communicating with parents, the small group almost always succeeds.

I give the same advice to every parish that's seeking to shift to small-group-based ministry: start one group at a time. Start small and grow big.

Establish same-gender groups of five to eight

Boys and girls mature at different paces. I've found that it's much easier to achieve transparency within a group if boys are with boys and girls are with girls. What's more, I strongly believe that boys learn to become men from the example of other men and that girls learn to become women from the example of other women.

Generally, I also recommend that groups start with five to eight members. Fewer than five can make it difficult to achieve the right dynamic, and more than eight can overwhelm discussion in the group.

Let discussions develop organically

Critical-thinking discussions generally come naturally to adults when they are respectful of one another and are mature enough to self-reflect. For young people, critical-thinking discussions don't always come naturally, and neither does self-reflection. This is why it's imperative to have small-group mentors who know how to help others engage in critical thinking.

Programmed questions don't generally work well. It would be difficult for me to give a small-group leader a list of questions, have him follow the plan exactly, and produce an excellent discussion. Excellent conversations happen organically. Small-group leaders should feel free to use tools or programs to help facilitate discussion but not rely on them so much that they kill discussion.

Create a comfortable environment

A comfortable environment is crucial for effective small-group discipleship. To be transparent with one another, young people need to feel comfortable. A living room, a coffee shop, a fireside room, a public hangout, and the outdoors are all conducive to creating an environment where trust and transparency can be developed.

The worst environment for a small-group meeting is the *parish* or a *classroom*. Parish halls are some of the least welcoming environments for teens (or for anyone, for that matter). I don't enjoy hanging out in an ugly, all-purpose parish hall, nor would

I bring my friends there to hang out. A classroom is an environment that is not associated with sharing—and teenagers won't be transparent in it.

My favorite place for small groups is the homes of teens. This may be considered taboo in some dioceses where safe-environment policies prevent meetings in homes. I would push back on these policies (but still comply with the safe-environment regulations in the diocese). The Vatican and our bishops have been stating for some time that faith formation starts with the domestic church—that is, the family. What kind of message are we sending if we say that small-group discipleship can't happen in a home? The home is where we want faith formation to happen—and we must be willing to bring formation to where teens are. I've found that leading my small group in homes also presents a tremendous opportunity to engage parents and to build trust and transparency with them.

Be flexible with scheduling group meetings

In parishes where I've run small-group discipleship, groups meet throughout the week when the teens' schedules allow for it. My small group meets during lunch period on Thursday at the high school. Another group meets on Friday evenings. Others meet after Mass on Sunday mornings. By providing flexibility, I have more teens engaged and more adults willing to volunteer.

Group teens with their friends

I once attended a diocesan youth rally with a small group of middle schoolers. The kids were split up and put into small groups with kids from other parishes. They were not allowed to be in small groups with their friends. I expressed my displeasure to the person in charge, and he responded, "It's good for them to get to know kids from other backgrounds and to share and learn about what they have in common." The problem is that the kids didn't share—they were not going to be transparent with total strangers.

If you gather into one room a group of strangers, chances are they won't share with each other the deep, intimate parts of their lives. We shouldn't expect teens to do this either. Teens need to be with people with whom they feel comfortable. They should be in groups with their natural friends.

Engage parents every week

Parents need to be involved in the discipleship of their teenagers. I don't tell the parents of my small group what is said in the group, but I do tell them the topics we're covering, and I try to connect with them every week. With all the tools and resources available for small-group leaders, it's easier than ever to engage parents as part of the discussion.

Many people have asked me whether I recommend having parents lead a small group with their own teenager in it. I think it would be difficult for parents to establish transparency with their own teens in their small group. As an alternative, if parents are engaged weekly in discussions with the small-group leader, the leader becomes a bridge for the parent and the teen, so that parents are informed and can continue ongoing discussion about the Faith at home.

Commit Your Parish to Real Change

Young people are leaving the Church because our current structures aren't meeting their pastoral needs.

We don't need more people trying to repair the failed paradigms and make them work.

We don't need more people trying to make the latest silver-bullet programs work.

We don't need more failed programs and large-group ministries that are excellent at getting our youth to participate but fail to develop lifelong disciples.

Our young people need mentors.

They need discipleship.

The tools exist to empower mentors, but we need our Church, our parishes, our schools, and our families to focus on developing mentors and putting them into relationships with teens in an environment where trust and transparency can develop.

We need forward thinkers who realize that we cannot repair the problems of youth ministry—we have to rebuild youth ministry.

The solutions are easier than we think—as long as we don't overcomplicate the problem. Our youth need their parents engaged in their lives. They need mentors and peers who will assist in meeting their pastoral needs. They don't need the latest fancy programs and youth groups. What they want is conversation, listening, and friendship. When our Church meets their basic needs, we will find that teens are hungry to become what our world needs: lifelong disciples of Jesus Christ.

Recommended Tools
and Resources

Small-group ministry is easier today than ever before because of the plethora of high-quality resources that have been developed for use in small groups. A small-group leader shouldn't feel as if he needs an advanced degree in theology in order to mentor teenagers. Without good tools and resources, he may feel unsupported in his ministry to teens. If he has excellent resources, he can feel empowered to mentor them because the resources help to develop the discussion, and the leader simply has to facilitate and share the wisdom of his own experience.

When using resources, I always tell my leaders, "We are not running a program. We are doing discipleship. This tool is intended to help you bring up and facilitate discussion." You need good tools if you want to build a house. But good tools are not enough: you need laborers to build the house as well. If your resources are used in the ways I have discussed throughout this book, then the resources will be effective. If your resources are used in the same ways that are not working, they won't be effective in making disciples.

Relationships and mentoring make disciples; programs do not. But tools can be useful in helping a mentor feel equipped to lead a small-group discussion with teenagers.

Here are several resources that I recommend:

St. Andrew Missionaries

St. Andrew Missionaries is an organization I started in 2016. The ministry serves parishes and dioceses that wish to develop small-group discipleship and family-based youth ministry. St. Andrew Missionaries recognizes that the "how to" is the hardest part of any ministry development plan. The ministry is committed to walking alongside parishes as they seek to shift their youth-ministry approach to youth discipleship. A list of seminars, workshops, on-site trainings, coaching packages, and other support resources can be found at www.standrewmissionaries.org.

FORMED and YDisciple

Video-based resources can be invaluable for small-group leaders because good videos are great discussion starters and video teachings take some of the pressure off small-group leaders to articulate the Faith effectively. FORMED is an online video-based subscription service that offers an enormous library of high-quality resources. These resources can be used in a variety of settings, including RCIA, Baptism preparation, marriage preparation, and adult faith formation.

One resource that I really like is YDisciple, which provides a series of short video studies (with leader guides and parent resources) in which discussion questions are specifically written to help develop small-group discussions. The leader guides tend to have more thought-provoking questions than your typical small-group resource, and the video clips are relatively short, allowing for the majority of small-group time to be spent in discussion. Because YDisciple resources are digital and live-streamed, the content of the discussion can be sent to parents every week to keep them informed about what the group is talking about.

YDisciple is available only with a FORMED subscription, which can be purchased through the Augustine Institute (www. augustineinstitute.org).

Ascension Press studies

Some of the best video resources are available through Ascension Press. Studies such as *Chosen*, *Altaration*, *You*, *Theology of the Body for Teens*, and the *Bible Timeline* are well done and present great content for discussion. Ascension Press also has a YouTube channel where you can find a tremendous amount of great video content (free!). High-quality videos can be great discussion starters for small groups and can take the burden of presenting content off the shoulders of a leader who may not have a complete catechetical background. Ascension Press also has its own digital library, free videos, and other resources, which can be found at www.evangelization.com.

Alpha

Alpha is a small-group program whose core teaching is the gospel. Like YDisciple, its resources are created to equip leaders in small-group discipleship, which makes the program more useful for the ministry structure I have discussed in this book.

Free video resources

If you work in a parish that has limited funds and you want to rely on video-based resources, there are many excellent places where you can get such resources free.

The Fellowship of Catholic University Students (FOCUS) has a great app called FOCUS Equip that provides a large number of Bible-study and video-based resources (https://focuson-campus.org/content/focus-equip-mobile-app). This app is used by many of the college missionaries who serve in small groups on campuses around the country and can be found in the App Store.

Real Life Catholic, an organization developed by Chris Stefanick, offers a variety of resources that introduce people to God's beauty, power, and truth. There are many tremendous, powerful video clips on its website (which are free!). They are great discussion starters for a small group.

Decision Point, developed by Matthew Kelly and the Dynamic Catholic organization, is another resource that's worth a look. It's a Confirmation program, and all its videos and leader guides are free.

Youth-ministry coaching organizations

Eric Gallagher's blog (http://discipleshipym.com/category/blog/) offers support for parishes and small-group mentors in the area of discipleship. Eric has helped many parishes develop small-group discipleship, and he regularly offers excellent advice on the subject. His organization, Discipleship Focused Youth Ministry, also provides training and seminars for parishes. Eric and Jim Beckman released a book in 2016 called *Discipleship Focused Youth Ministry*.

I also highly recommend Chris Wesley's Marathon Youth Ministry (christopherwesley.org) and Chris Bartlett's Next Level Ministry (nextlevelministry.org). Both of these men have excellent youth-ministry backgrounds in small-group discipleship, and they provide coaching services for parishes.

Book studies

Never underestimate the power of an excellent book. Simply reading and discussing one — chapter by chapter — can be an excellent discipleship group task. Dynamic Catholic offers many excellent low-priced books. You can also use classics written by authors such as C. S. Lewis and G. K. Chesterton. A lectionary-based Bible study can be very effective in a discipleship group — especially if the person who is mentoring has a good grasp of the Bible.

Bibliography

Augustine Institute. "5 Fundamental Needs of Teenagers," in *YDisciple Handbook*, 5. Denver: Augustine Institute, 2015.

Clark, Chap. *Hurt 2.0: Inside the World of Today's Teenagers*. Grand Rapids, MI: Baker Academic, 2011.

DeVries, Mark. *Family-Based Youth Ministry*. 2nd ed. Downers Grove, IL: InterVarsity Press, 2004.

Francis. Apostolic exhortation *Evangelii Gaudium: Apostolic Exhortation*. November 24, 2013.

Gray, Mark M., Mary L. Gautier, and Melissa A. Cidade. *The Changing Face of U.S. Catholic Parishes*. Washington, DC: National Association for Lay Ministry, 2011.

Neal, Meghan. "1 in 12 Teens Have Attempted Suicide." *Daily News*, June 9, 2012. http://www.nydailynews.com/life-style/health/1-12-teens-attempted-suicide-report-article-1.1092622.

Pulkkinen, Levi. "Eastside Catholic Vice Principal Ousted after Gay Marriage Drops Lawsuit." *SeattlePI*, November 28, 2014. http://www.seattlepi.com/local/article/Vice-principal-ousted-for-Eastside-Catholic-after-5919802.php.

Smith, Christian, and Melinda Lundquist Denton. *Soul Searching: The Religious and Spiritual Lives of American Teenagers.* Oxford: Oxford University Press, 2005.

Smith, Peter Jesserer. "Diocese to Lose $2 Million in Teacher's IVF Lawsuit." National Catholic Register, December 27, 2014. http://www.ncregister.com/daily-news/diocese-to-lose-2-million-in-teachers-ivf-lawsuit.

Weddell, Sherry A. *Forming Intentional Disciples: The Path to Knowing and Following Jesus.* Huntington, IN: Our Sunday Visitor, 2012.

Weigel, George. *Witness to Hope: The Biography of Pope John Paul II.* New York: Cliff Street Books, 1999.

About the Author

Everett Fritz is the founder and executive director of St. Andrew Missionaries. He holds an MA in theology from the Augustine Institute and a BA in theology from Franciscan University of Steubenville. He authored the best-selling book *Freedom: Battle Strategies for Conquering Temptation*—a guide for young men trapped in the shackles of sexual sin. Everett regularly speaks on the topics of discipleship, youth evangelization, and chastity. He and his wife, Katrina, reside in Denver with their children.

Sophia Institute

Sophia Institute is a nonprofit institution that seeks to nurture the spiritual, moral, and cultural life of souls and to spread the Gospel of Christ in conformity with the authentic teachings of the Roman Catholic Church.

Sophia Institute Press fulfills this mission by offering translations, reprints, and new publications that afford readers a rich source of the enduring wisdom of mankind.

Sophia Institute also operates two popular online Catholic resources: CrisisMagazine.com and CatholicExchange.com.

Crisis Magazine provides insightful cultural analysis that arms readers with the arguments necessary for navigating the ideological and theological minefields of the day. *Catholic Exchange* provides world news from a Catholic perspective as well as daily devotionals and articles that will help you to grow in holiness and live a life consistent with the teachings of the Church.

In 2013, Sophia Institute launched Sophia Institute for Teachers to renew and rebuild Catholic culture through service to Catholic education. With the goal of nurturing the spiritual, moral, and cultural life of souls, and an abiding respect for the role and work of teachers, we strive to provide materials and programs that are at once enlightening to the mind and ennobling to the heart; faithful and complete, as well as useful and practical.

Sophia Institute gratefully recognizes the Solidarity Association for preserving and encouraging the growth of our apostolate over the course of many years. Without their generous and timely support, this book would not be in your hands.

www.SophiaInstitute.com
www.CatholicExchange.com
www.CrisisMagazine.com
www.SophiaInstituteforTeachers.org

Sophia Institute Press® is a registered trademark of Sophia Institute. Sophia Institute is a tax-exempt institution as defined by the Internal Revenue Code, Section 501(c)(3). Tax I.D. 22-2548708.